Hilarious Silly Joke Book For Kids Age 7-11

This Book Belongs To

,,,,,,,,,,,,,,,,,,,,,,,,,,,,,,,,

* Why did the tomato blush?
<u>Because it saw the salad dressing.</u>

* Why didn't the duck pay for the lip balm?
<u>He wanted to put it on his bill.</u>

* What do you call an alligator in a vest?
<u>An investigator!</u>

* Why did Darth Vader turn off one light?
<u>He prefers it on the dark side.</u>

* Why did Darth Vader turn off one light?
<u>He prefers it on the dark side.</u>

* What do you call a fly without wings?
<u>A walk.</u>

* Why did the boy throw a clock out the window?
<u>To see time fly.</u>

* What's black and white and red all over?
<u>An embarrassed zebra.</u>

* Why is Cinderella bad at soccer?
Because she runs away from the ball.

* What did one eye say to the other?
Between us, something smells.

* What's faster hot or cold?
Hot, because everyone catches a cold.

* How do you throw a party on Mars?
You planet.

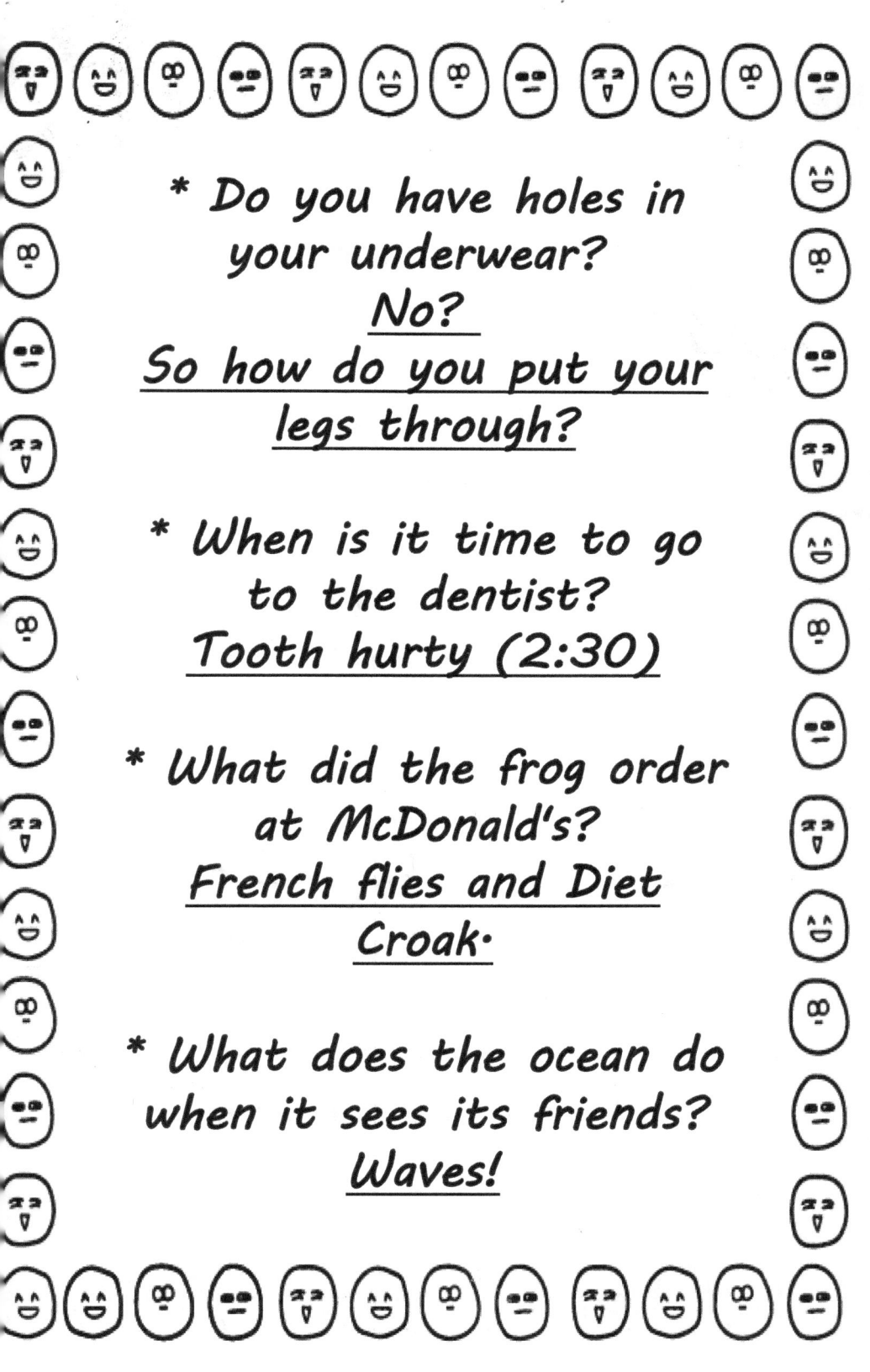

* Do you have holes in your underwear?
<u>No?</u>
<u>So how do you put your legs through?</u>

* When is it time to go to the dentist?
<u>Tooth hurty (2:30)</u>

* What did the frog order at McDonald's?
<u>French flies and Diet Croak.</u>

* What does the ocean do when it sees its friends?
<u>Waves!</u>

* Knock, knock…
Who's there?
Tank.
Tank who?
You're welcome.

* Knock, knock…
Who's there?
Boo.
Boo who?
Why are you crying?

* Why did the girl throw a stick of butter out the window?
To see butter-fly.

* Did you hear about the two guys who stole a calendar?
They both got 6 months.

* Why didn't the teddy bear eat dessert?
Because he was stuffed.

* How do you make a tissue dance?
Put a little boogie in it.

* How did Darth Vader know what Luke Skywalker got him for his birthday?
He felt his presents.

* What's green, has six legs, and if it drops out of a tree onto you will kill you?
<u>A pool table.</u>

* What do you call cheese that doesn't belong to you?
Nacho cheese!

* Where do cows go for entertainment?
<u>The mooooooooovies.</u>

* Be careful when walking your dog... <u>you might step in a Poo...dle.</u>

* How do you learn to be a trash collector?
<u>Just pick it up as you go along.</u>

* What would a bear say if he got confused?
<u>I barely understand.</u>

*What do bumblebees chew?
<u>Bumble gum</u>

* Why was 6 afraid of 7?
<u>Because 7, 8 (ate), 9.</u>

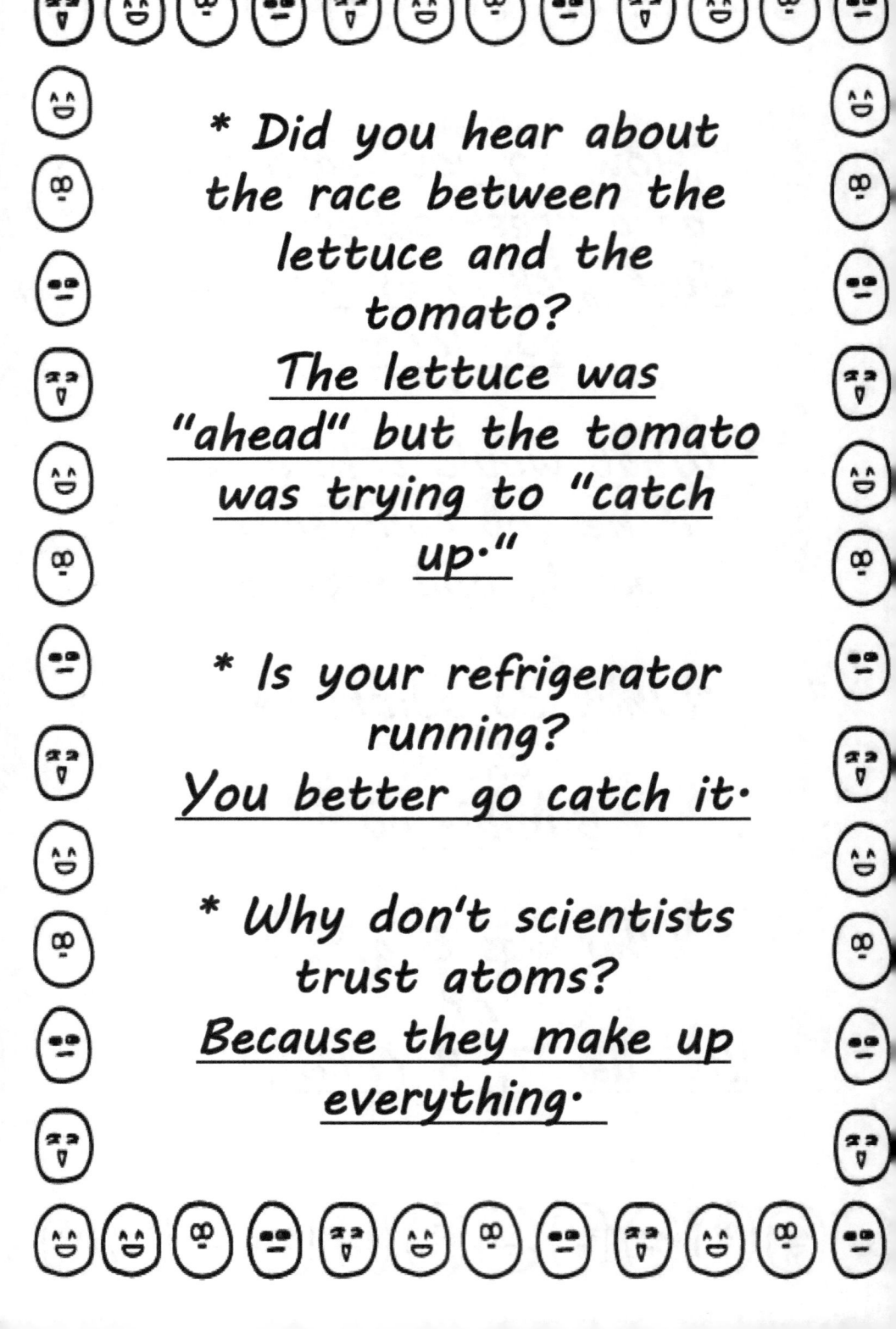

* Did you hear about the race between the lettuce and the tomato?
The lettuce was "ahead" but the tomato was trying to "catch up."

* Is your refrigerator running?
You better go catch it.

* Why don't scientists trust atoms?
Because they make up everything.

* What's a pirate's favorite subject in school?
<u>Arrrrrrrrrt.</u>

* Knock, knock...
Who's there?
<u>Cows go.</u>
Cows go who?
<u>No silly, cows go moo.</u>

* Will you remember me a year from now?
<u>Yes.</u>
Will you remember me tomorrow?
<u>Yes.</u>
Will you remember me when you grow old?
<u>Yes.</u>

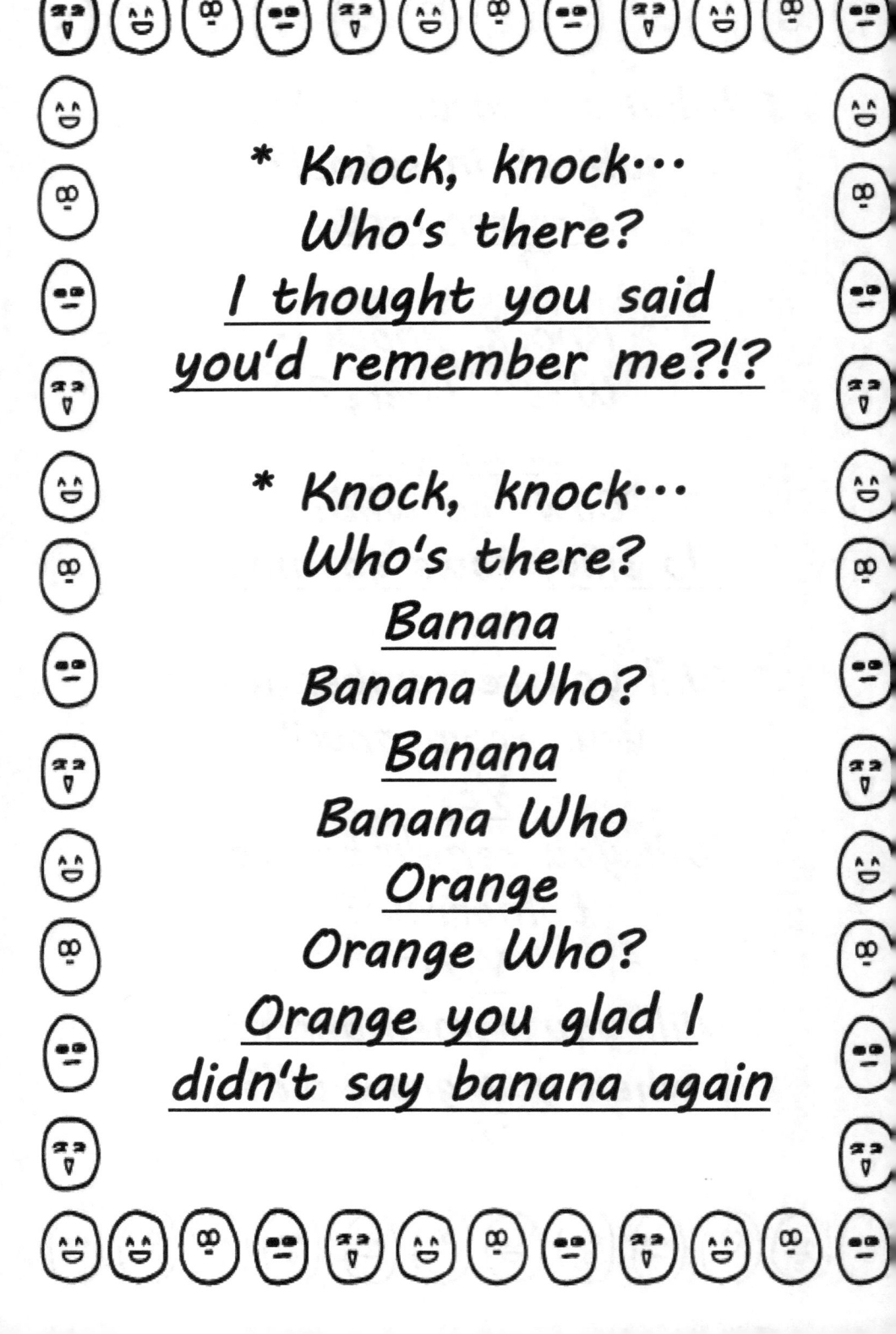

* Knock, knock…
Who's there?
<u>I thought you said you'd remember me?!?</u>

* Knock, knock…
Who's there?
<u>Banana</u>
Banana Who?
<u>Banana</u>
Banana Who
<u>Orange</u>
Orange Who?
<u>Orange you glad I didn't say banana again</u>

* Knock, knock...
Who's there?
<u>Dwyane</u>
Dwyane who?
<u>Dwyane the bathtub.</u>

* Knock, knock...
Who's there? <u>Owls say.</u>
<u>Owls say who? Yes, they do.</u>

*What's the smartest insect? <u>A spelling bee!</u>

*Name the kind of tree you can hold in your hand? <u>A palm tree!</u>

*Why do birds fly south in the winter? <u>It's faster than walking!</u>

*Which superhero hits home runs? <u>Batman!</u>

*Why did the bird get in trouble at school? <u>For tweeting on a test!</u>

*What kind of math do birds love? <u>Owl-gebra!</u>

*Which planet loves to sing? <u>Nep-tune!</u>

*Why are basketball courts always wet? <u>Because the players dribble!</u>

*What kind of keys are sweet? <u>Cookies!</u>
<u>Knock, knock!</u>

*Who's there?
<u>Woo.</u>
<u>Woo-hoo!</u>
<u>No need to get so excited; it's just a joke!</u>

*What do you call cheese that belongs to someone else? <u>Nacho cheese!</u>

*Why did the peanut get into a rocket? <u>He wanted to be an astro-nut!</u>

*What fruit do twins love? <u>Pears!</u>

*How do bees brush their hair? <u>With honeycombs!</u>

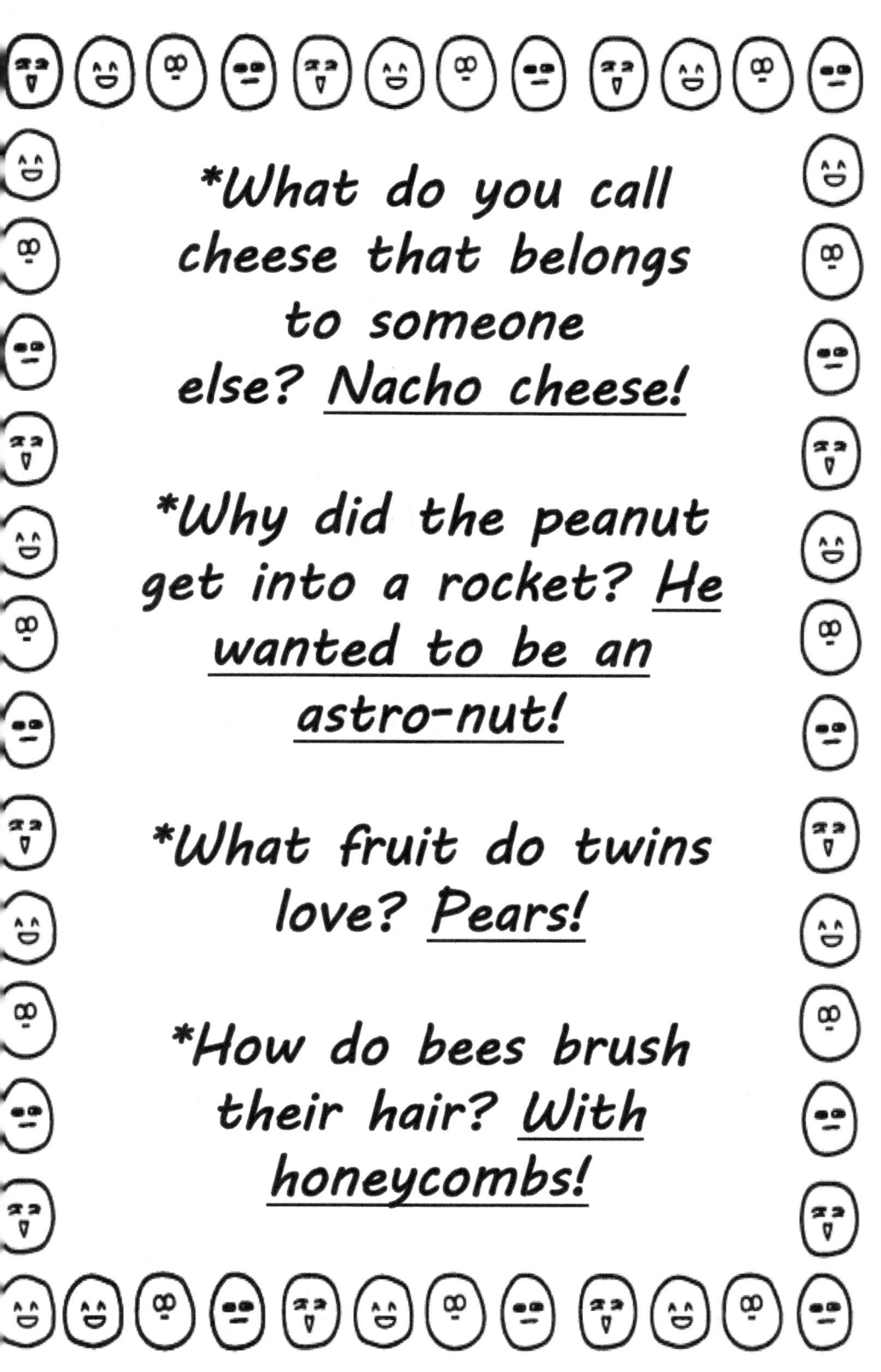

*Why won't peanut butter tell you a secret? <u>He's afraid you'll spread it!</u>

*Who eats snails? <u>People who don't like fast food!</u>

*Why did the banana visit the doctor? <u>He wasn't peeling well!</u>

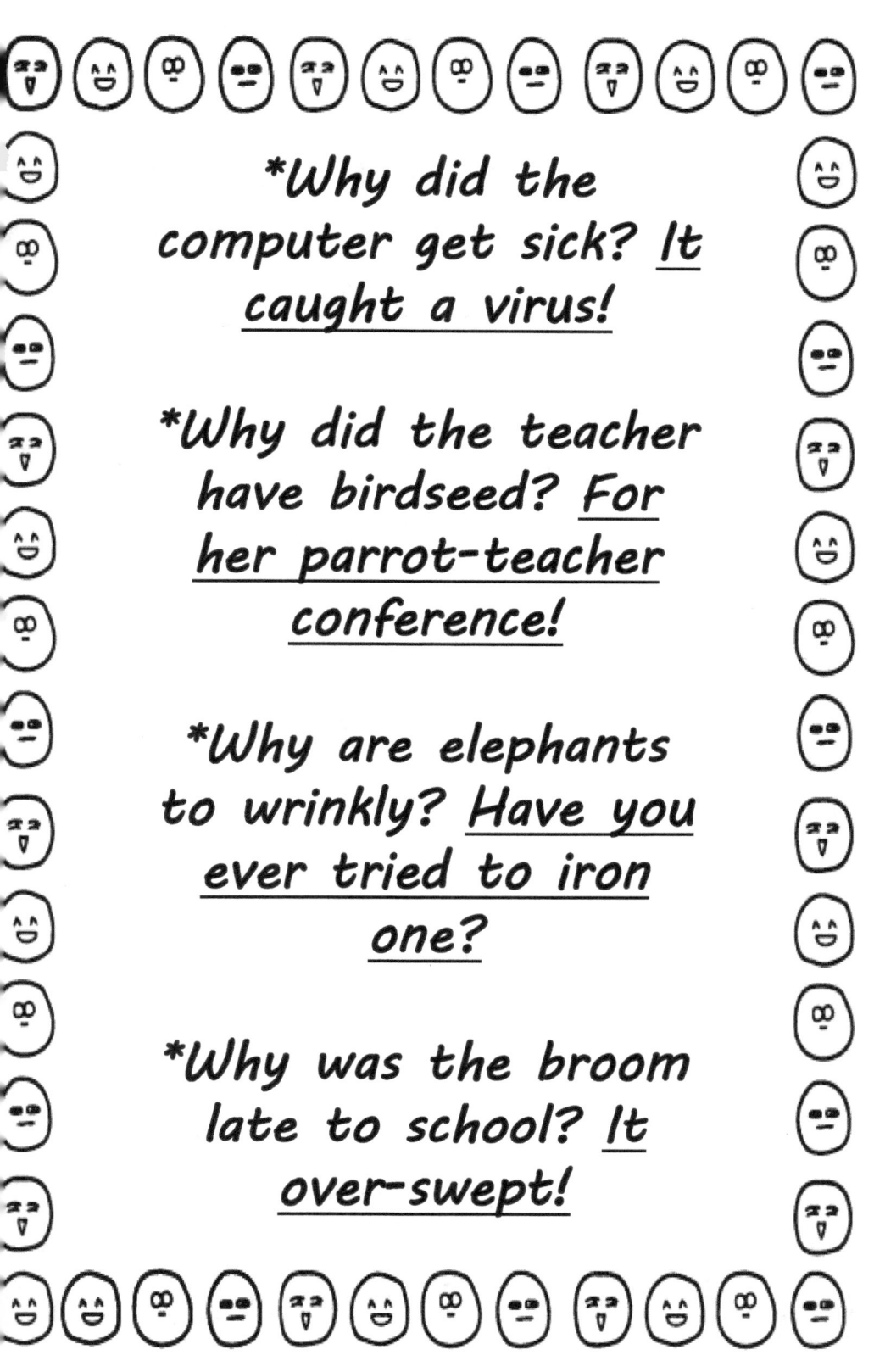

*Why did the computer get sick? It caught a virus!

*Why did the teacher have birdseed? For her parrot-teacher conference!

*Why are elephants to wrinkly? Have you ever tried to iron one?

*Why was the broom late to school? It over-swept!

* What does a vampire take for a sore throat? <u>Coffin drops.</u>

*What is the strongest animal in the sea? <u>Mussels!</u>

*What kind of chicken is the funniest? <u>A comedi-hen!</u>

*What do you call a seagull that lives by the bay? <u>A bagel!</u>

*What color do cats prefer? <u>Purr-ple</u>

*What does a triceratops sit on? <u>Its tricera-bottom!</u>

*What is a sleeping dinosaur? <u>A dino-snore!</u>

*What kind of pizza do dogs eat? <u>Pup-eroni pizza!</u>

*How do you help a baby astronaut fall asleep? <u>You rock-et!</u>

*If cars run on gas, what do cats run on? Their paws!

*What do cats wear to bed? Paw-jamas!

*What kind of pictures do turtles take? Shell-fies!

*What do you call a famous turtle? A shell-ebrity!

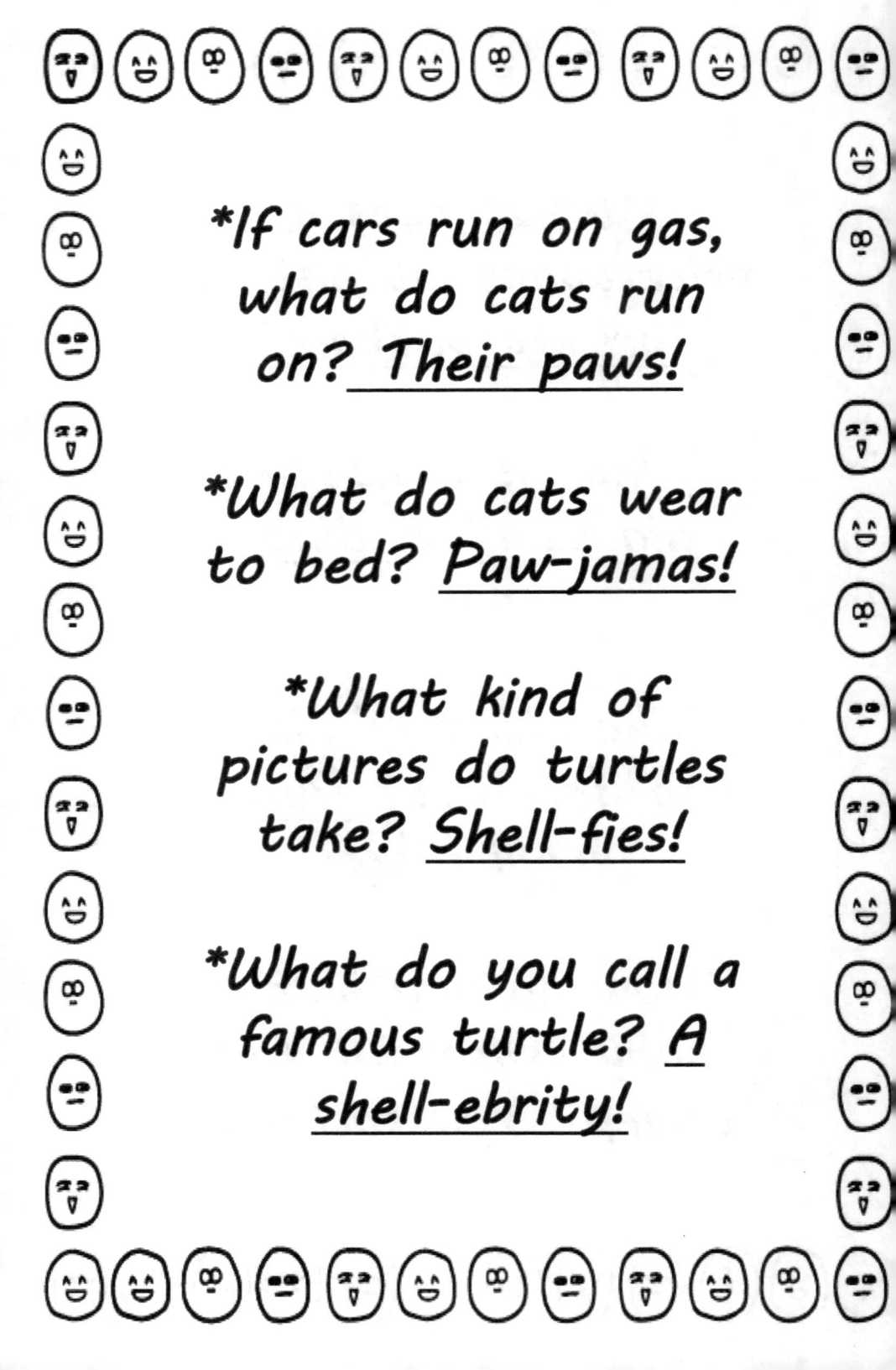

*What do you feed an alligator? Anything it wants!

*What makes a sick lemon feel better? Lemon-aid!

*How does Spiderman do research? On the World Wide Web!

*What's the largest gem on earth? A baseball diamond!

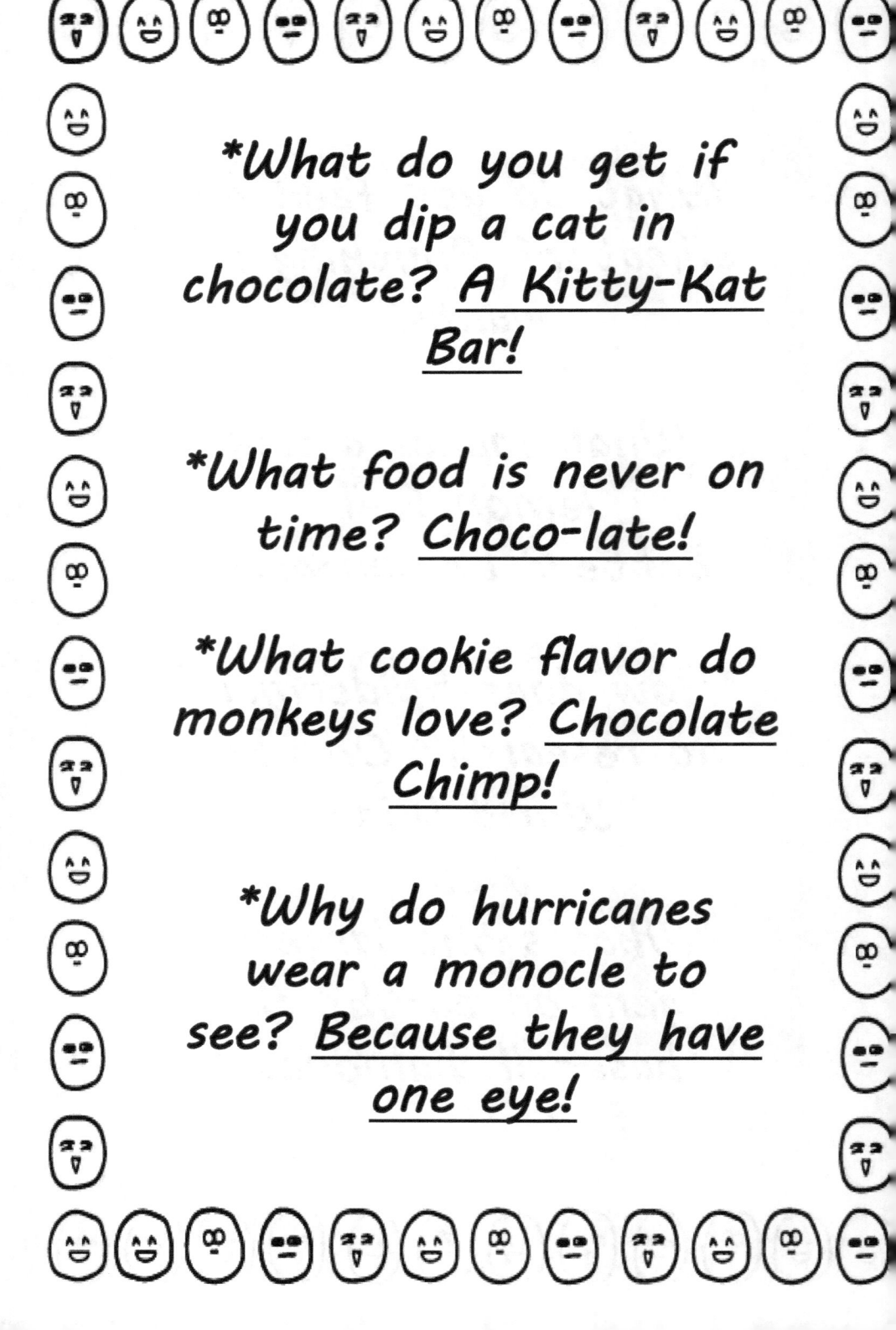

*What do you get if you dip a cat in chocolate? A Kitty-Kat Bar!

*What food is never on time? Choco-late!

*What cookie flavor do monkeys love? Chocolate Chimp!

*Why do hurricanes wear a monocle to see? Because they have one eye!

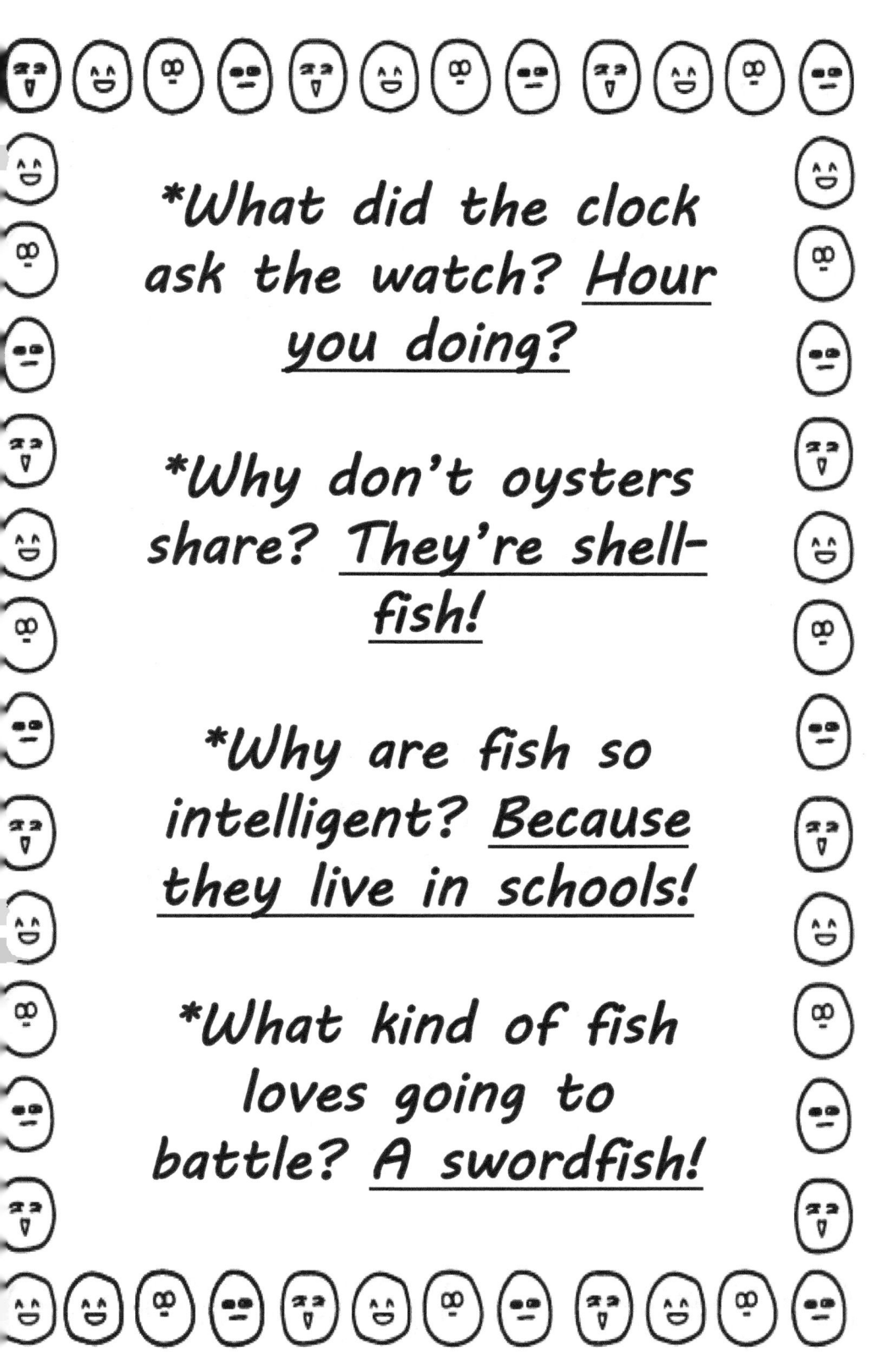

*What did the clock ask the watch? <u>Hour you doing?</u>

*Why don't oysters share? <u>They're shell-fish!</u>

*Why are fish so intelligent? <u>Because they live in schools!</u>

*What kind of fish loves going to battle? <u>A swordfish!</u>

*Where do birds invest their money? <u>The stork-market!</u>

*What nut has the most money? <u>A cashew!</u>

*What do you call a cow who plays the trumpet? <u>A moo-sician!</u>

*What's a pirate's favorite county? <u>Arrrrgh-entina!</u>

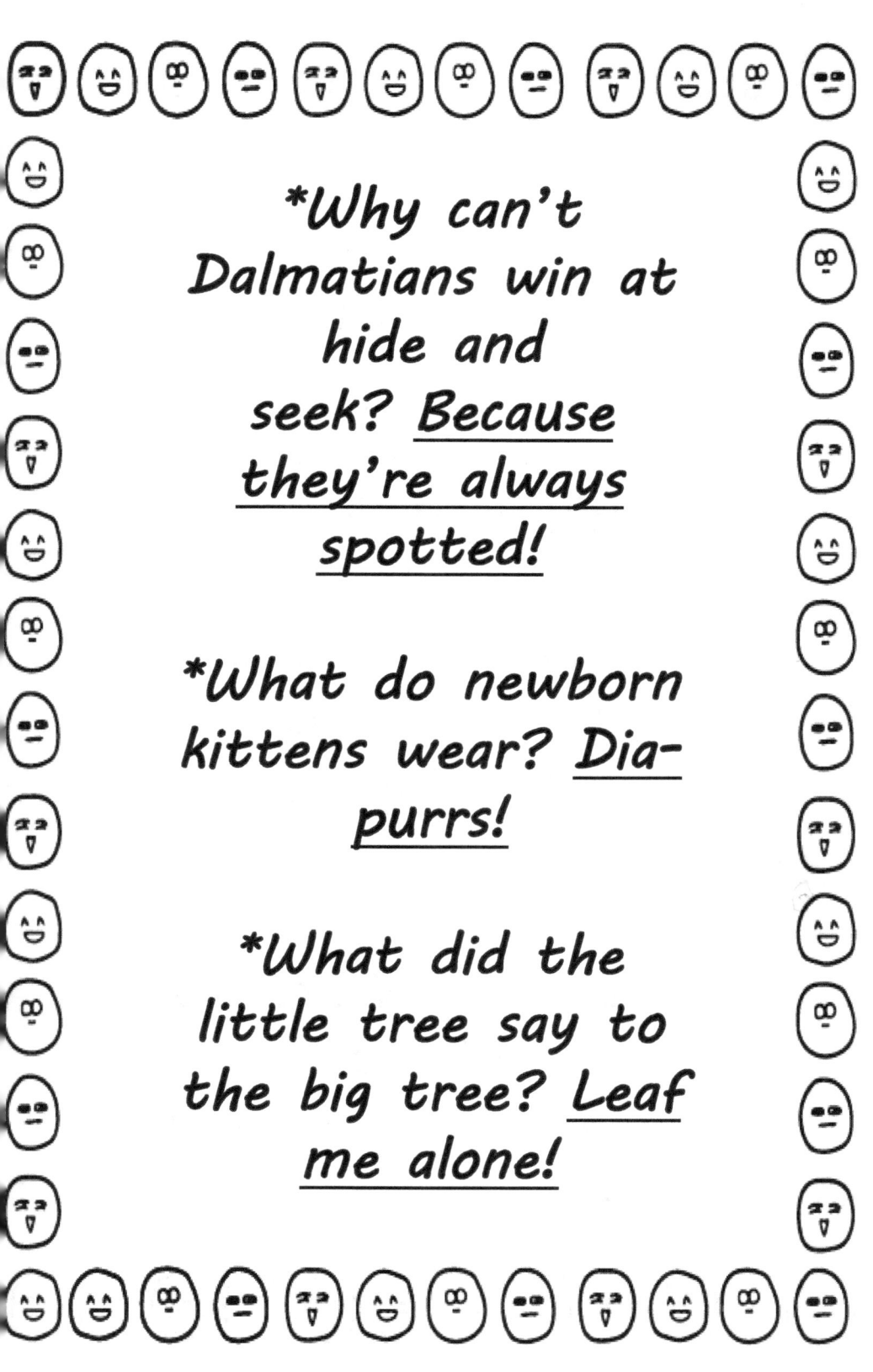

*Why can't Dalmatians win at hide and seek? <u>Because they're always spotted!</u>

*What do newborn kittens wear? <u>Dia-purrs!</u>

*What did the little tree say to the big tree? <u>Leaf me alone!</u>

*Knock, knock!
Who's there?
<u>Tank.</u>
Tank who?
<u>You're welcome!</u>

*What's in the recipe for gold soup? <u>Fourteen carrots!</u>

*Name Spiderman's favorite month? <u>Web-ruary!</u>

*Knock, knock!
Who's there?
Figs.
Figs who?
<u>Figs the doorbell! It's broken!</u>

*Why are ducks good at basketball? <u>They make fowl shots!</u>

*What kind of dog always knows the time? <u>A watch-dog!</u>

*What goes up and never comes down? <u>Your age!</u>

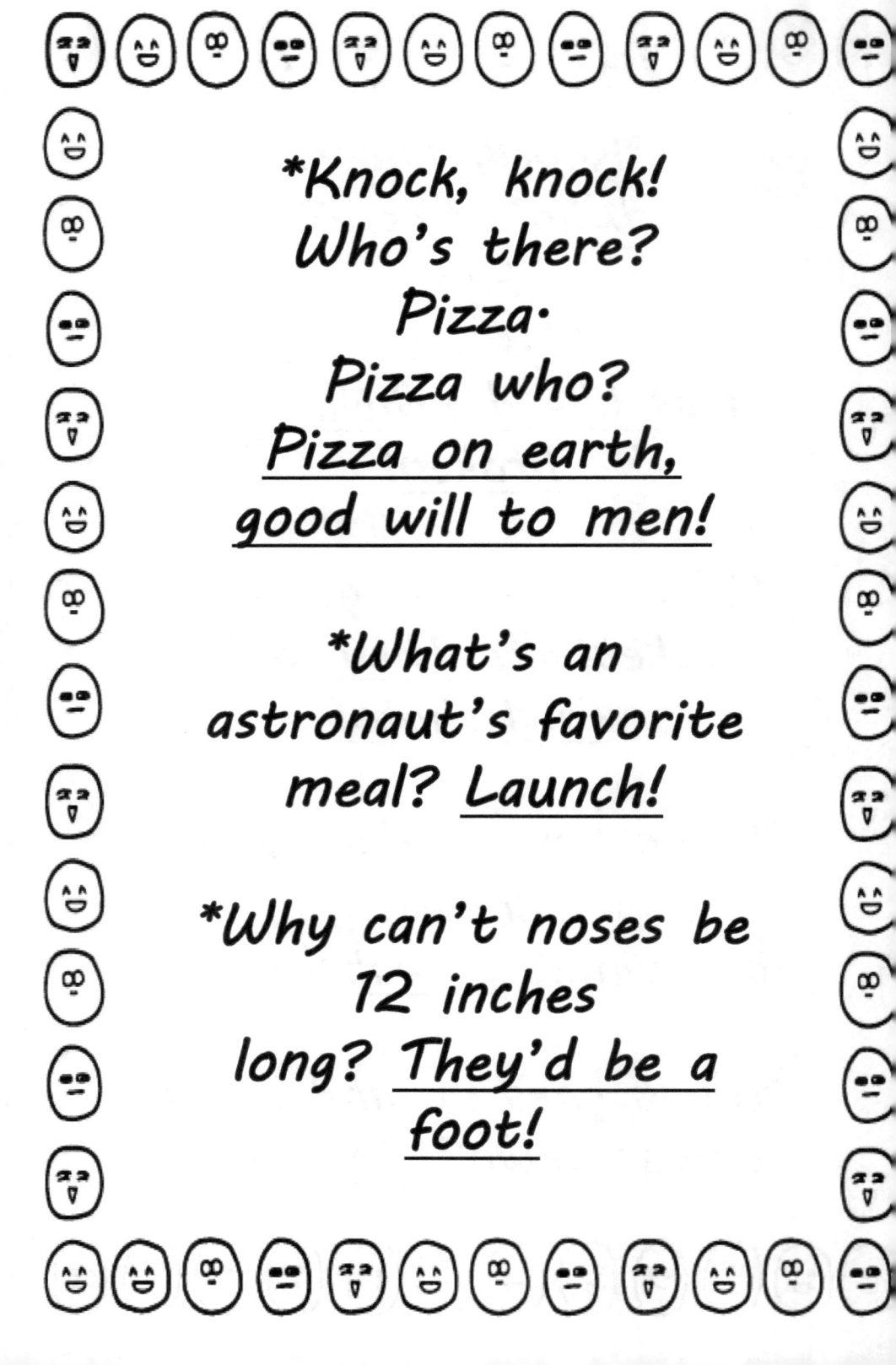

*Knock, knock!
Who's there?
Pizza.
Pizza who?
<u>Pizza on earth, good will to men!</u>

*What's an astronaut's favorite meal? <u>Launch!</u>

*Why can't noses be 12 inches long? <u>They'd be a foot!</u>

*What does it sound like when a nut sneezes? <u>Ca-shew!</u>

*Where do smart burgers sit? <u>On honor rolls!</u>

*Which holiday do cows enjoy most? <u>Moo-Year's Day!</u>

*Why can't bicycles stand on on their own? <u>They're two-tired!</u>

*Where do you go to school to learn how to greet people? <u>Hi school!</u>

*What do cheerleaders eat for breakfast? <u>Cheerios!</u>

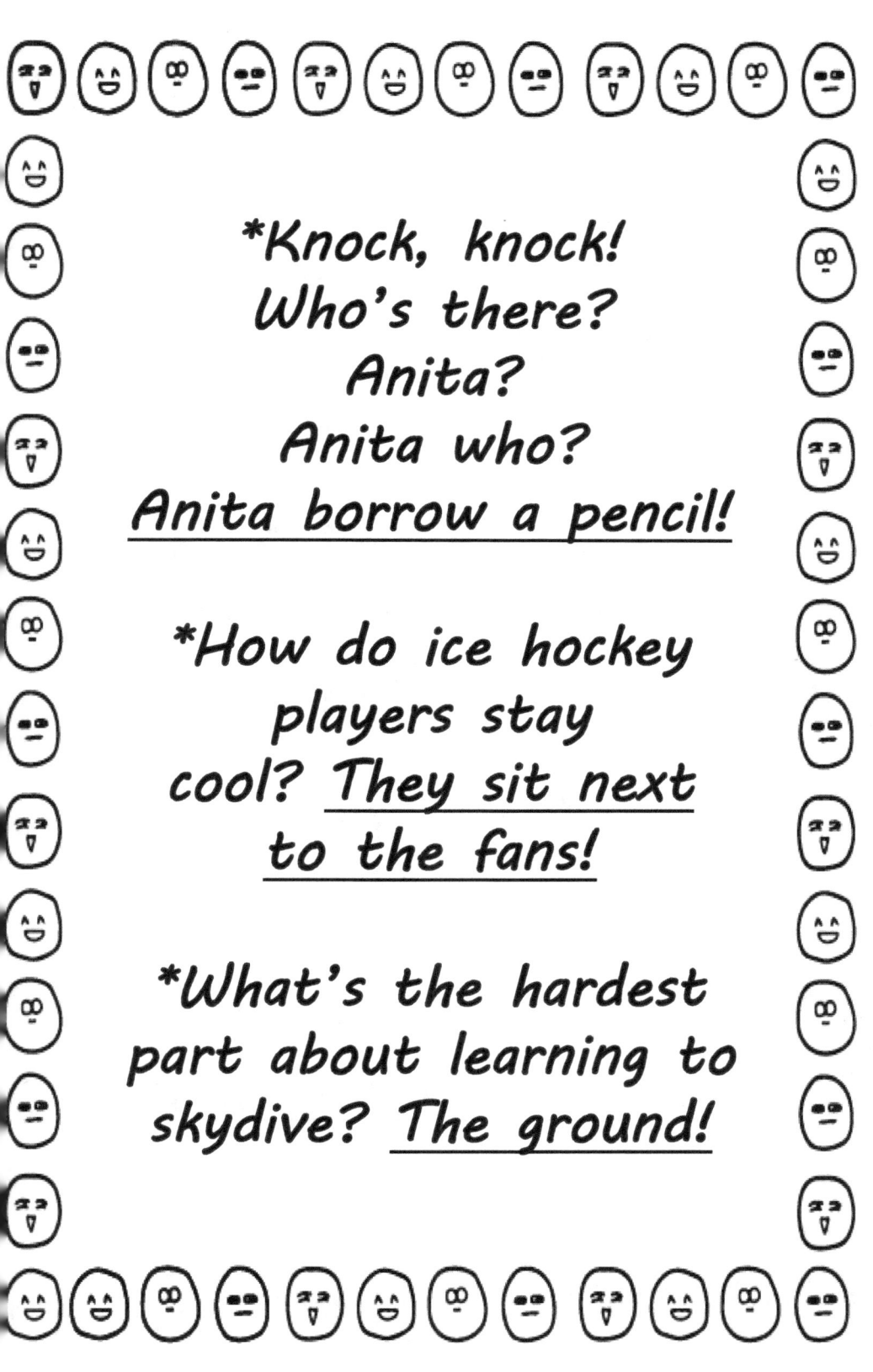

*Knock, knock!
Who's there?
Anita?
Anita who?
Anita borrow a pencil!

*How do ice hockey players stay cool? They sit next to the fans!

*What's the hardest part about learning to skydive? The ground!

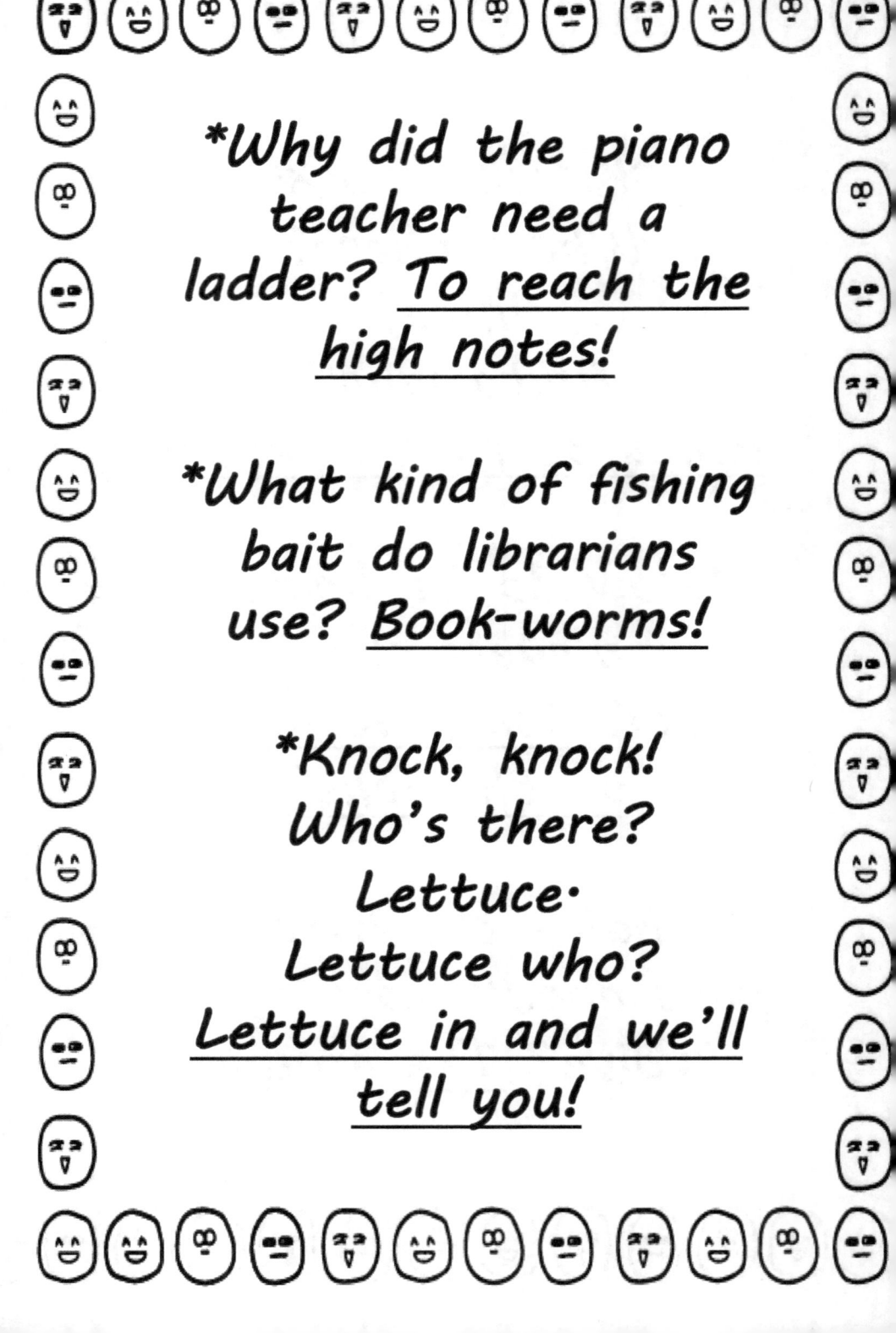

*Why did the piano teacher need a ladder? <u>To reach the high notes!</u>

*What kind of fishing bait do librarians use? <u>Book-worms!</u>

*Knock, knock!
Who's there?
Lettuce.
Lettuce who?
<u>Lettuce in and we'll tell you!</u>

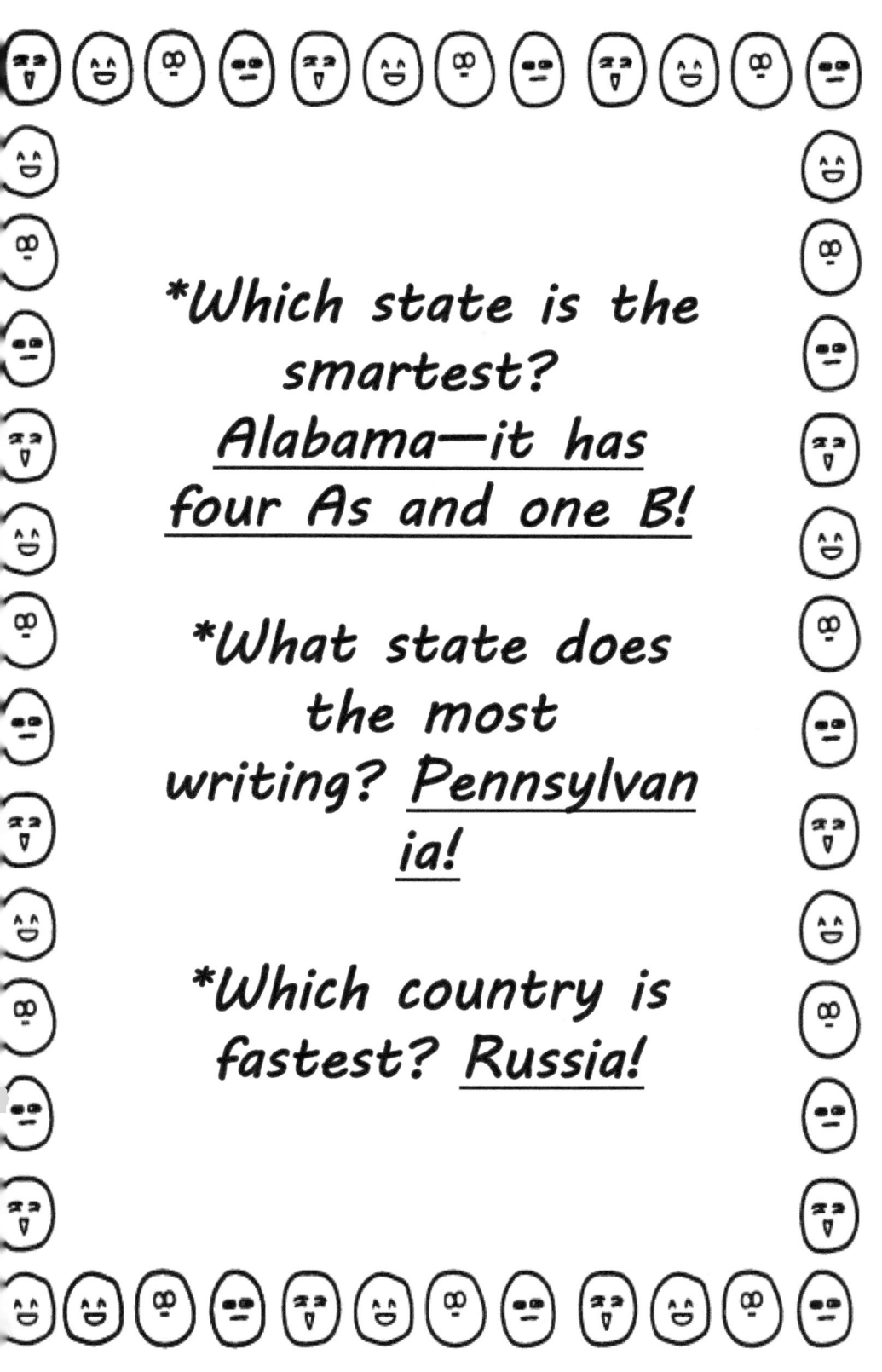

*Which state is the smartest? <u>Alabama—it has four As and one B!</u>

*What state does the most writing? <u>Pennsylvania!</u>

*Which country is fastest? <u>Russia!</u>

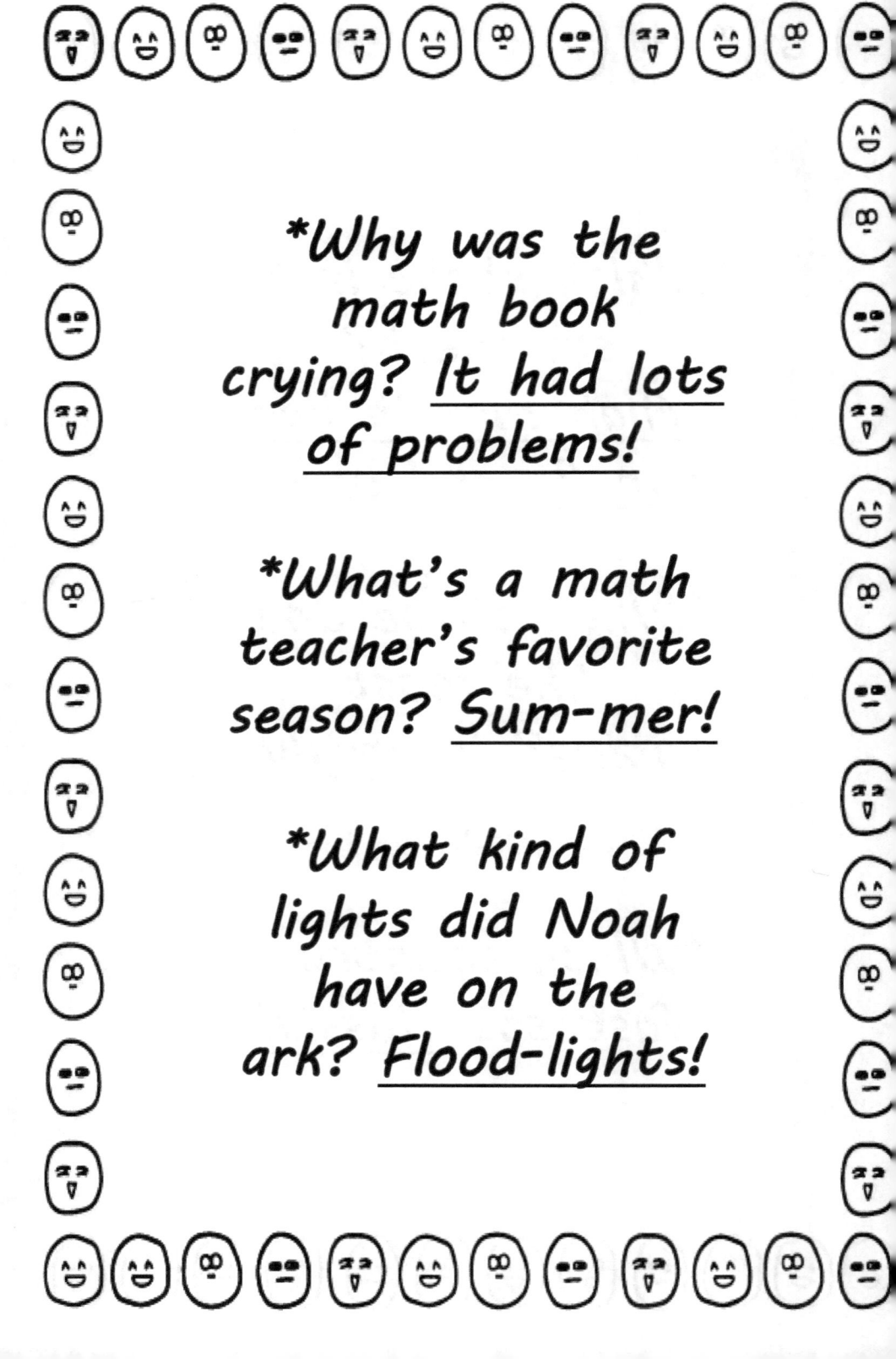

*Why was the math book crying? It had lots of problems!

*What's a math teacher's favorite season? Sum-mer!

*What kind of lights did Noah have on the ark? Flood-lights!

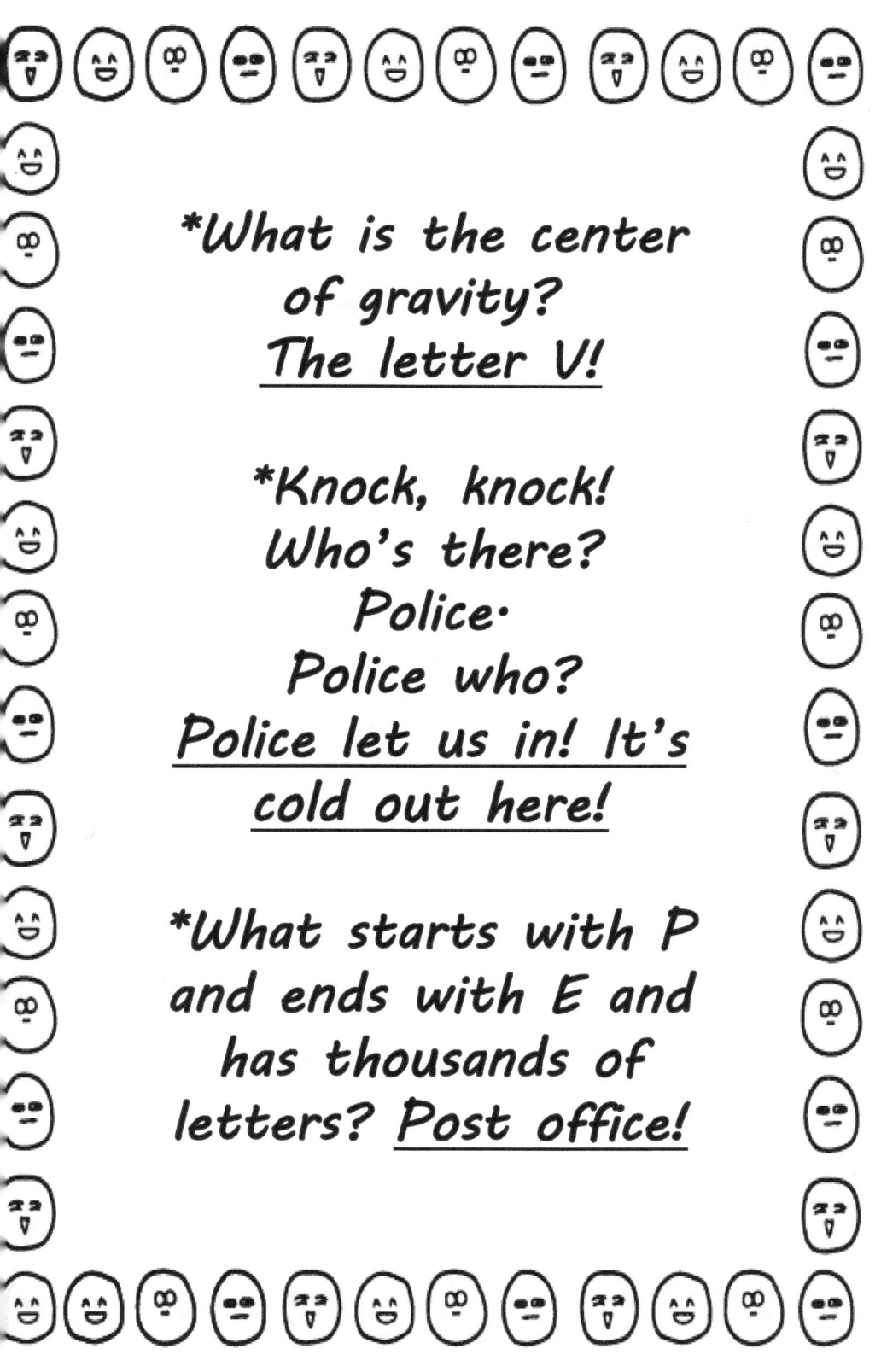

*What is the center of gravity?
<u>The letter V!</u>

*Knock, knock!
Who's there?
Police.
Police who?
<u>Police let us in! It's cold out here!</u>

*What starts with P and ends with E and has thousands of letters? <u>Post office!</u>

*What breaks when you speak?
<u>Silence!</u>

*What do attorneys wear to court?
<u>Law-suits!</u>

*What's the most famous fish?
<u>A starfish!</u>

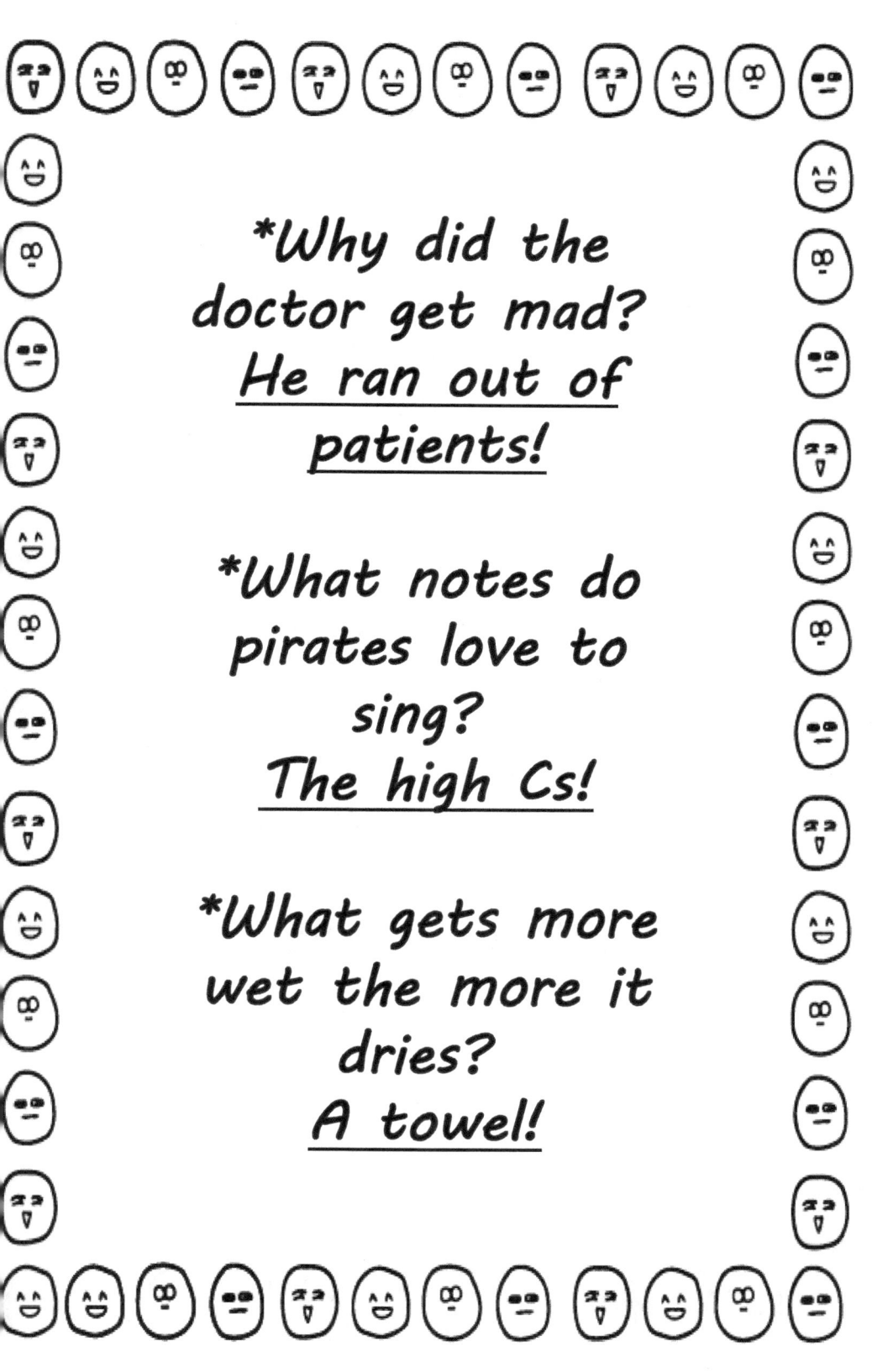

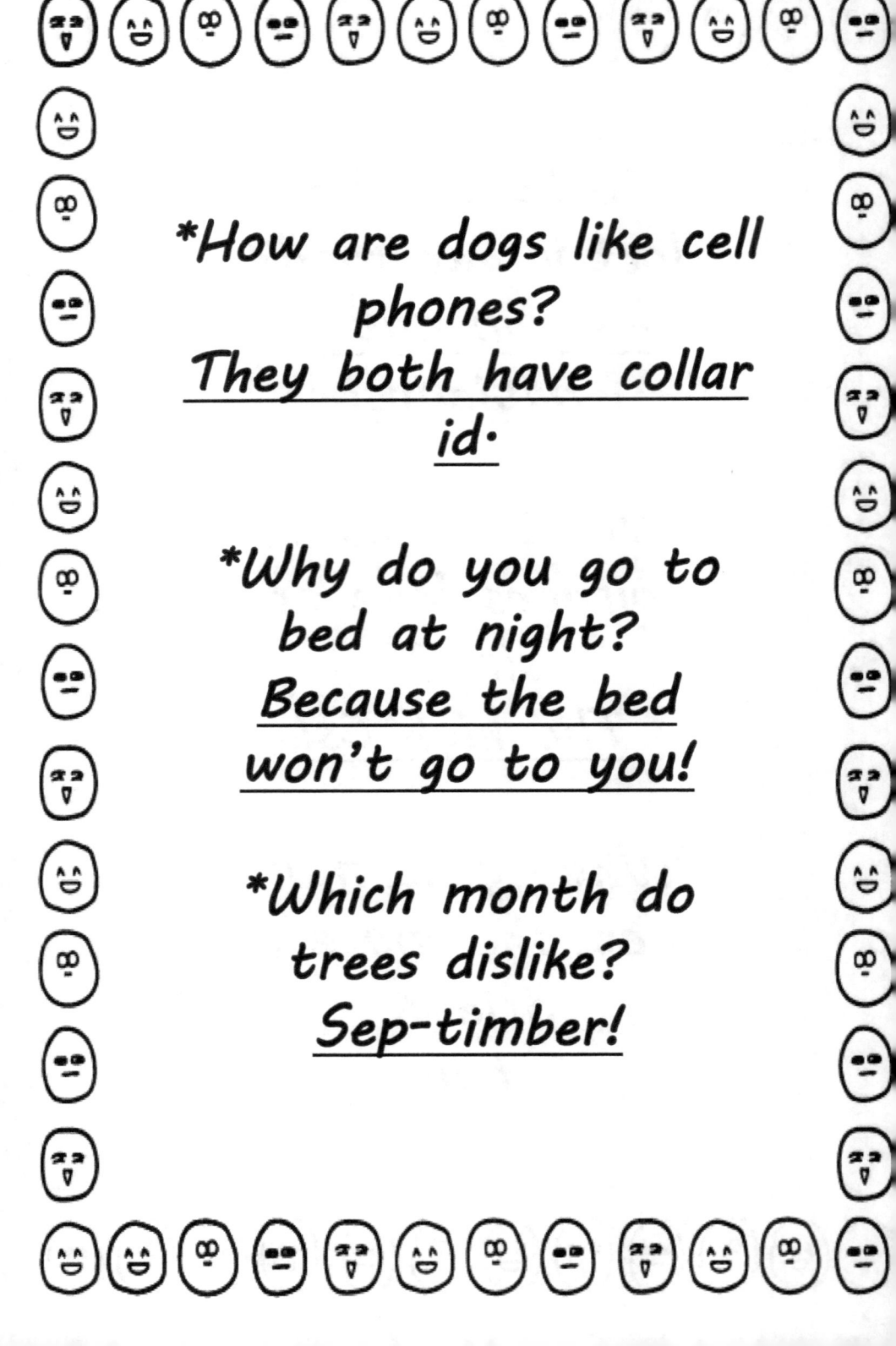

*How are dogs like cell phones?
<u>They both have collar id.</u>

*Why do you go to bed at night?
<u>Because the bed won't go to you!</u>

*Which month do trees dislike?
<u>Sep-timber!</u>

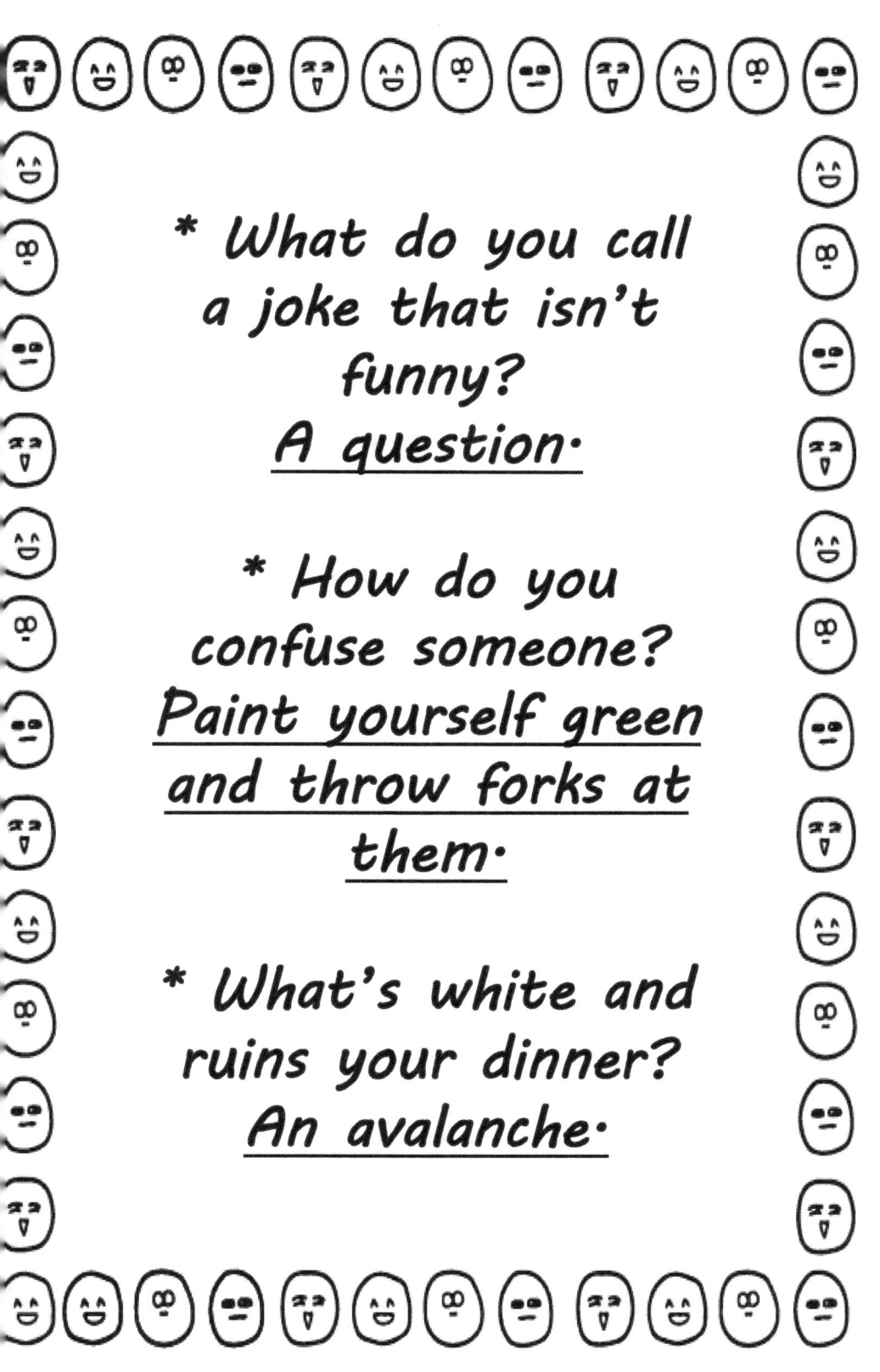

* What do you call a joke that isn't funny?
<u>A question.</u>

* How do you confuse someone?
<u>Paint yourself green and throw forks at them.</u>

* What's white and ruins your dinner?
<u>An avalanche.</u>

* What's red and shaped like a bucket?
<u>A red bucket.</u>

* How do you turn a soup to gold?
<u>Add 24 carrots.</u>

* What looks like a tree, and has wheels?
<u>A tree, I lied about the wheels.</u>

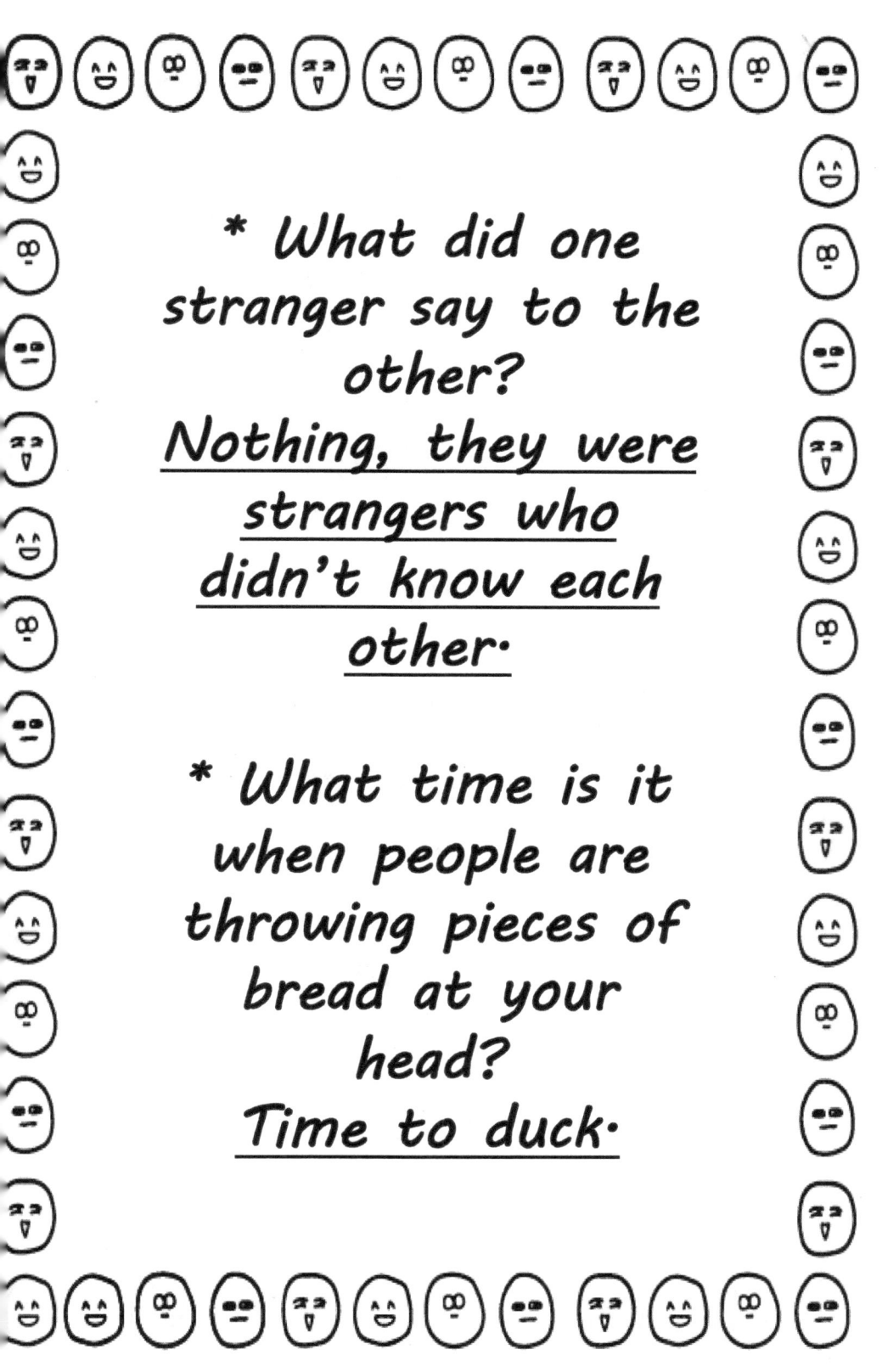

* What did one stranger say to the other?
Nothing, they were strangers who didn't know each other.

* What time is it when people are throwing pieces of bread at your head?
Time to duck.

* Why did the God of Thunder need to stretch his muscles so much when he was a kid?
<u>He was a little Thor.</u>

* Why were there more birds flying on one side of the V formation than the other?
<u>Because the other side had fewer birds.</u>

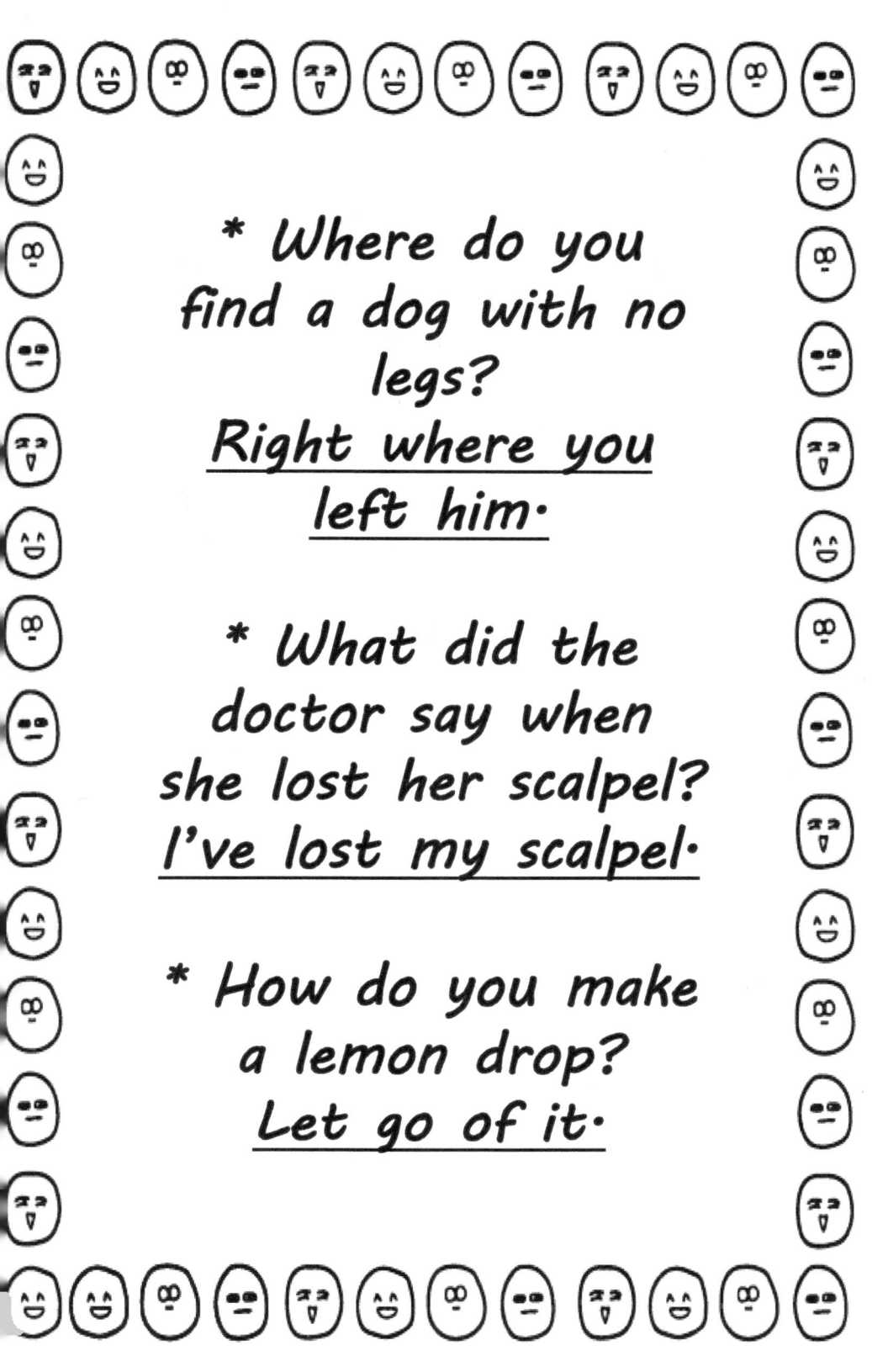

* Where do you find a dog with no legs?
<u>Right where you left him.</u>

* What did the doctor say when she lost her scalpel?
<u>I've lost my scalpel.</u>

* How do you make a lemon drop?
<u>Let go of it.</u>

* A proton, an electron, and an ion went into a restaurant.
<u>But nobody noticed because all three are microscopic.</u>

* Why didn't the dinosaur eat the baby?
Because dinosaurs became extinct before humans existed.

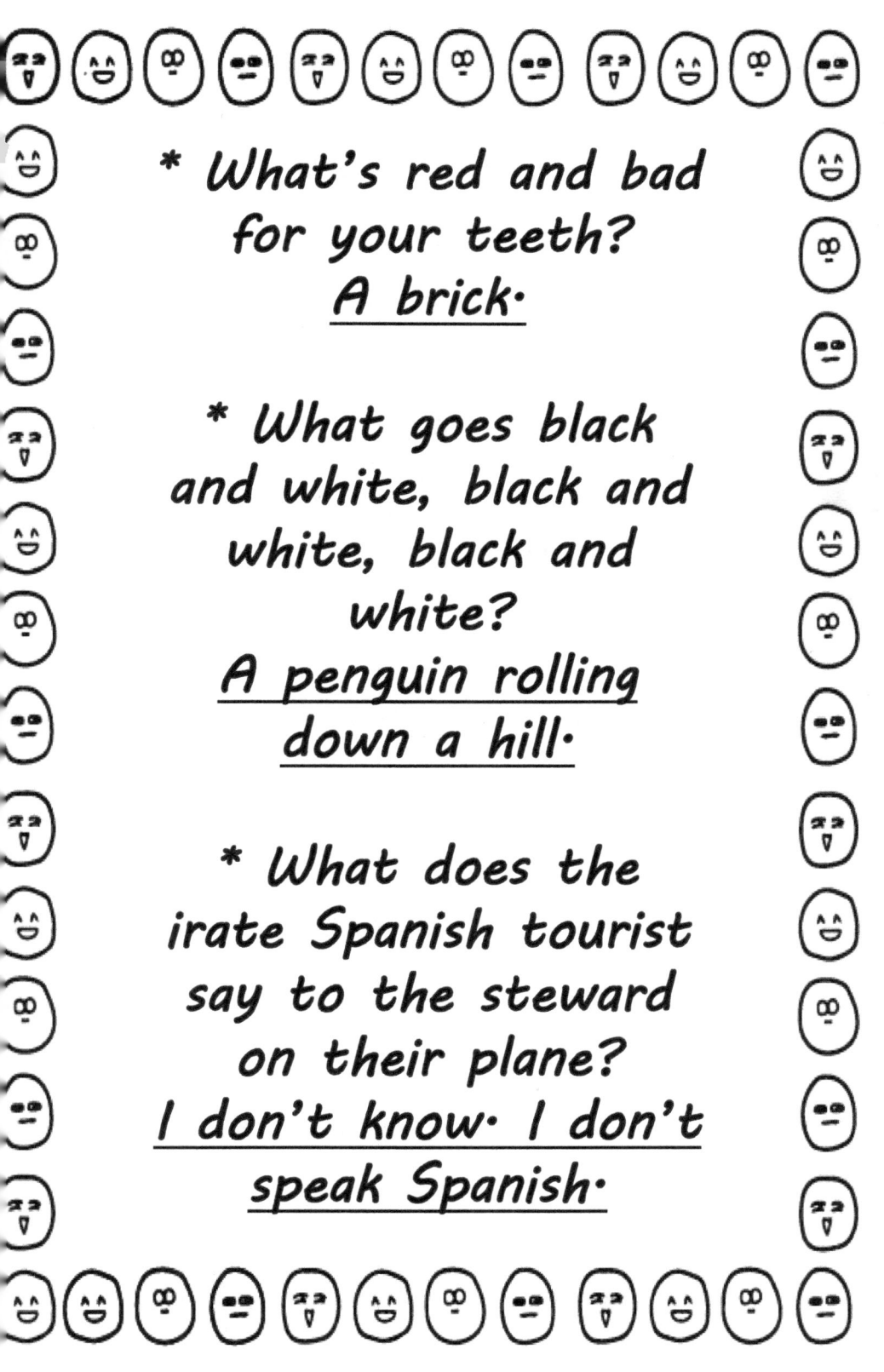

* What's red and bad for your teeth?
<u>A brick.</u>

* What goes black and white, black and white, black and white?
<u>A penguin rolling down a hill.</u>

* What does the irate Spanish tourist say to the steward on their plane?
<u>I don't know. I don't speak Spanish.</u>

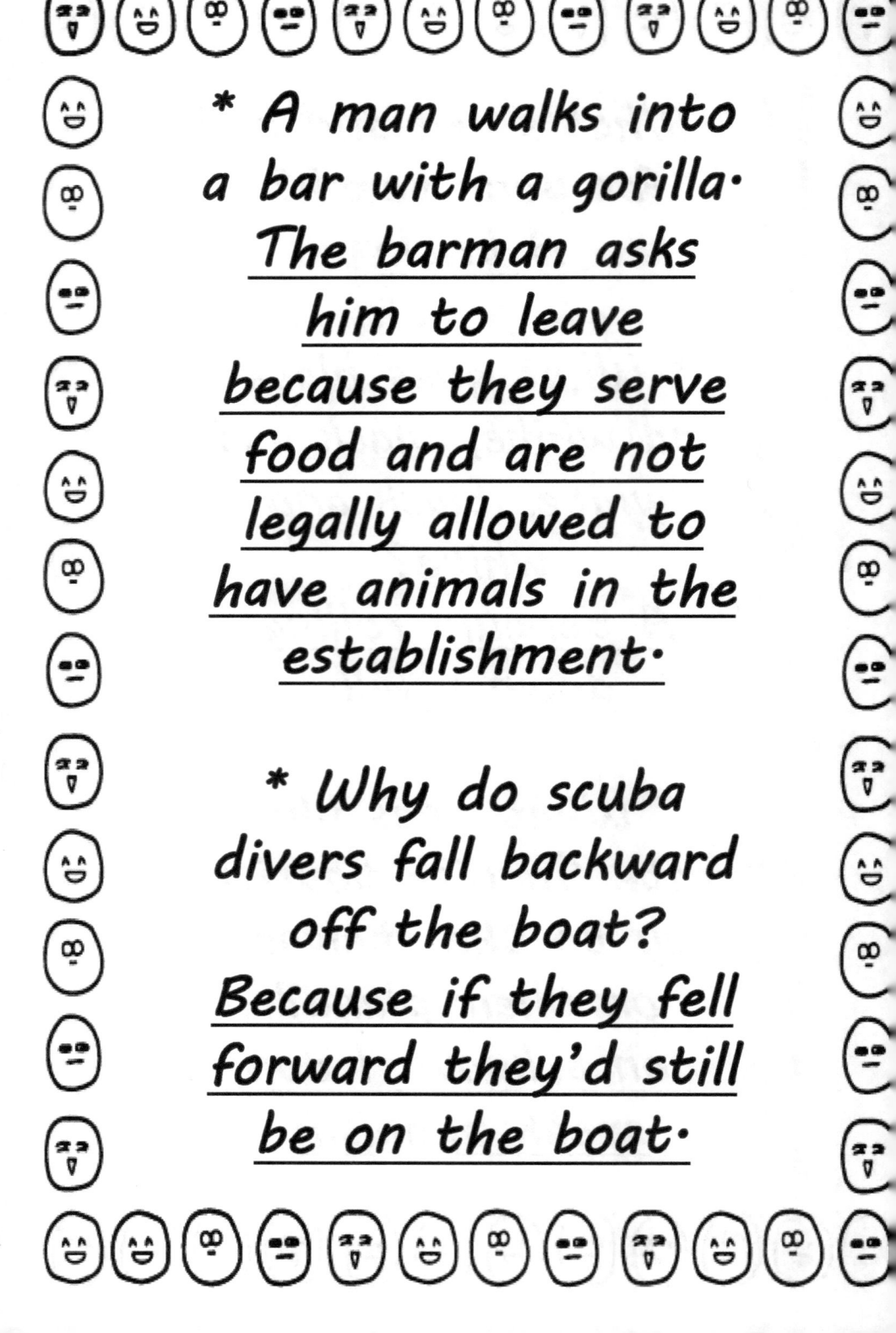

* A man walks into a bar with a gorilla. <u>The barman asks him to leave because they serve food and are not legally allowed to have animals in the establishment.</u>

* Why do scuba divers fall backward off the boat? <u>Because if they fell forward they'd still be on the boat.</u>

* What did Tarzan say when he saw the herd of hippos? <u>Look, a herd of hippos.</u>

* Where do frogs keep their money? <u>In a riverbank.</u>

* Why can't a pig keep a secret? <u>Because they always end up squealing.</u>

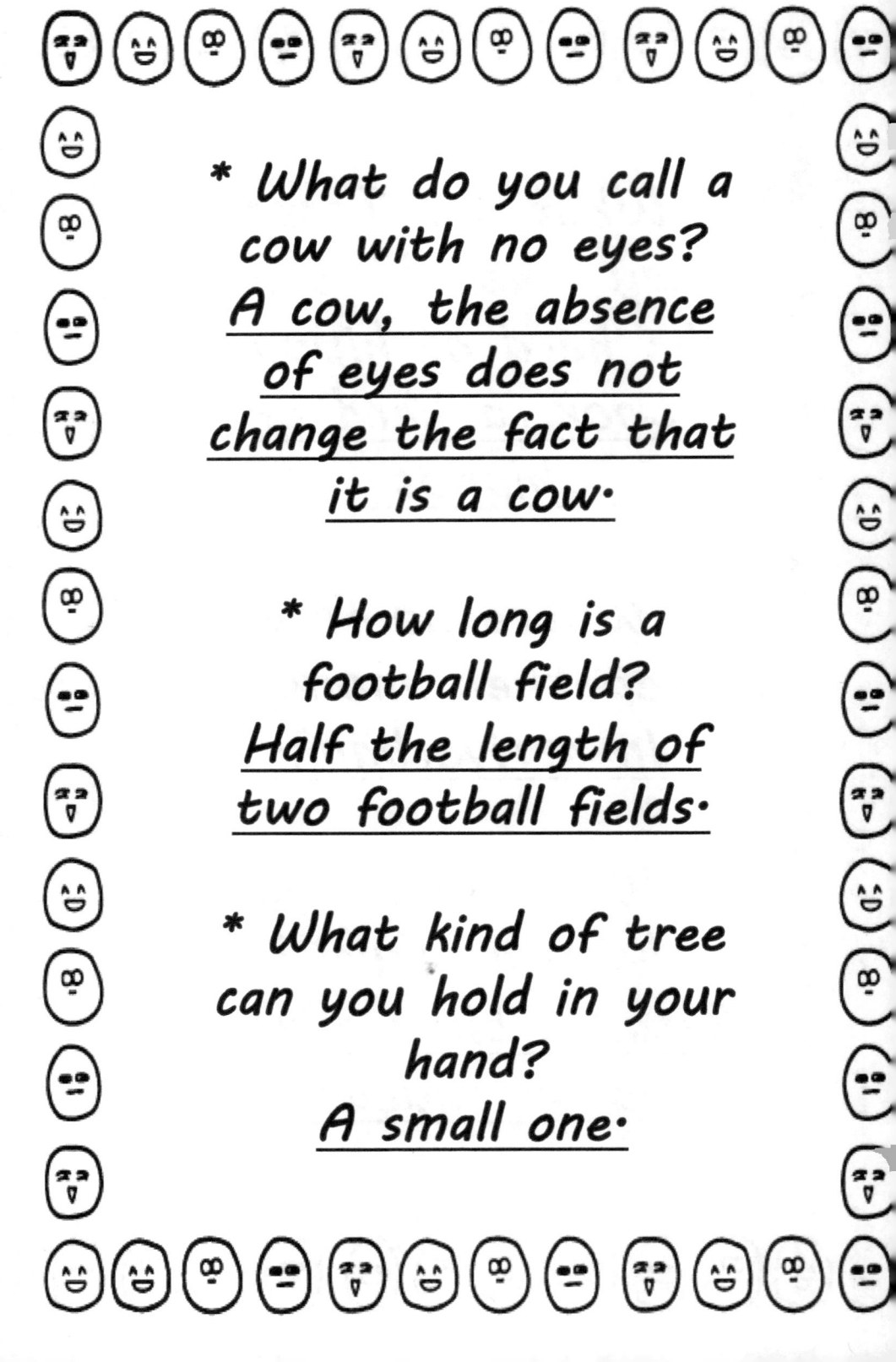

* What do you call a cow with no eyes?
<u>A cow, the absence of eyes does not change the fact that it is a cow.</u>

* How long is a football field?
<u>Half the length of two football fields.</u>

* What kind of tree can you hold in your hand?
<u>A small one.</u>

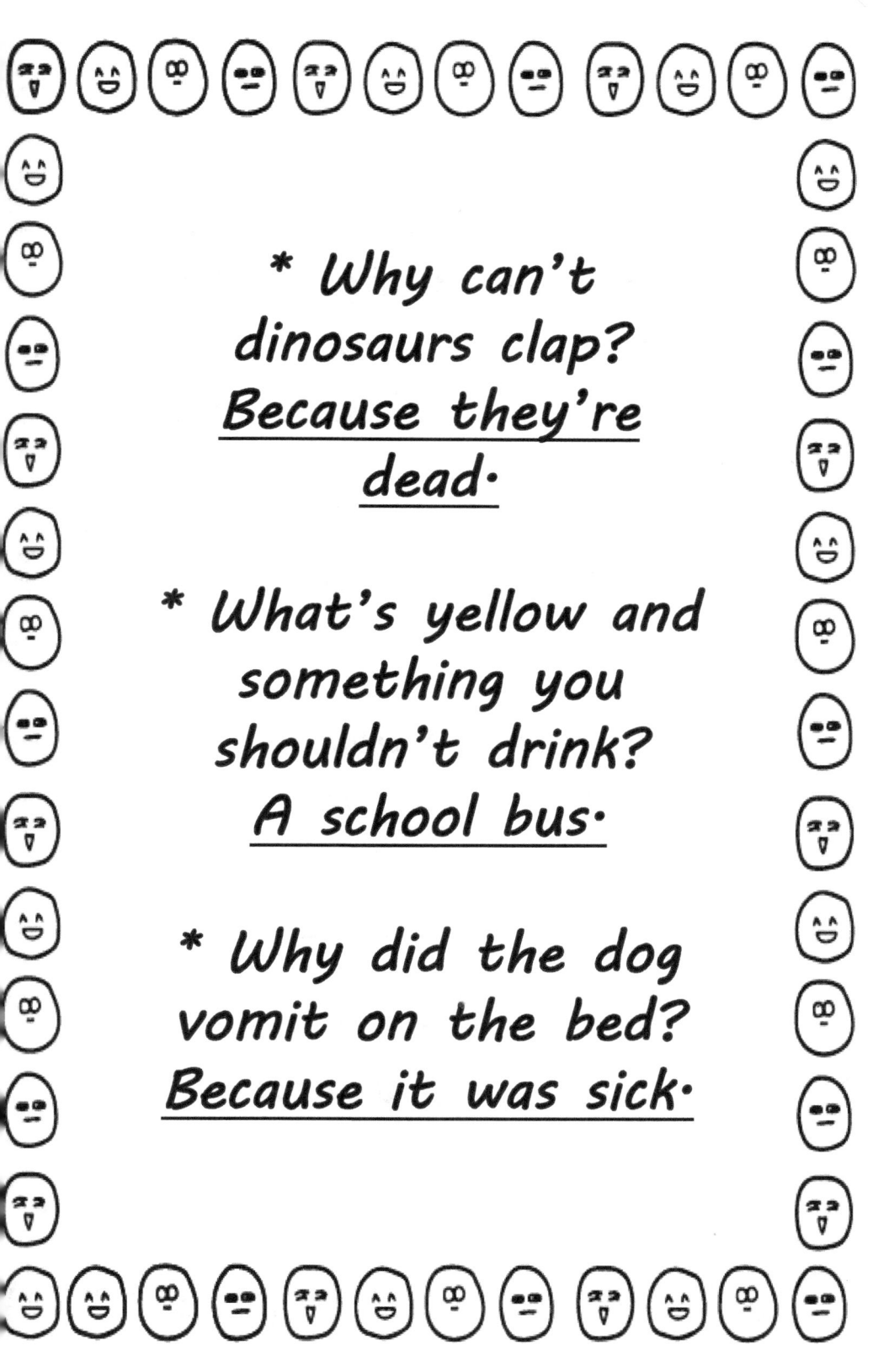

* Why can't dinosaurs clap? <u>Because they're dead.</u>

* What's yellow and something you shouldn't drink? <u>A school bus.</u>

* Why did the dog vomit on the bed? <u>Because it was sick.</u>

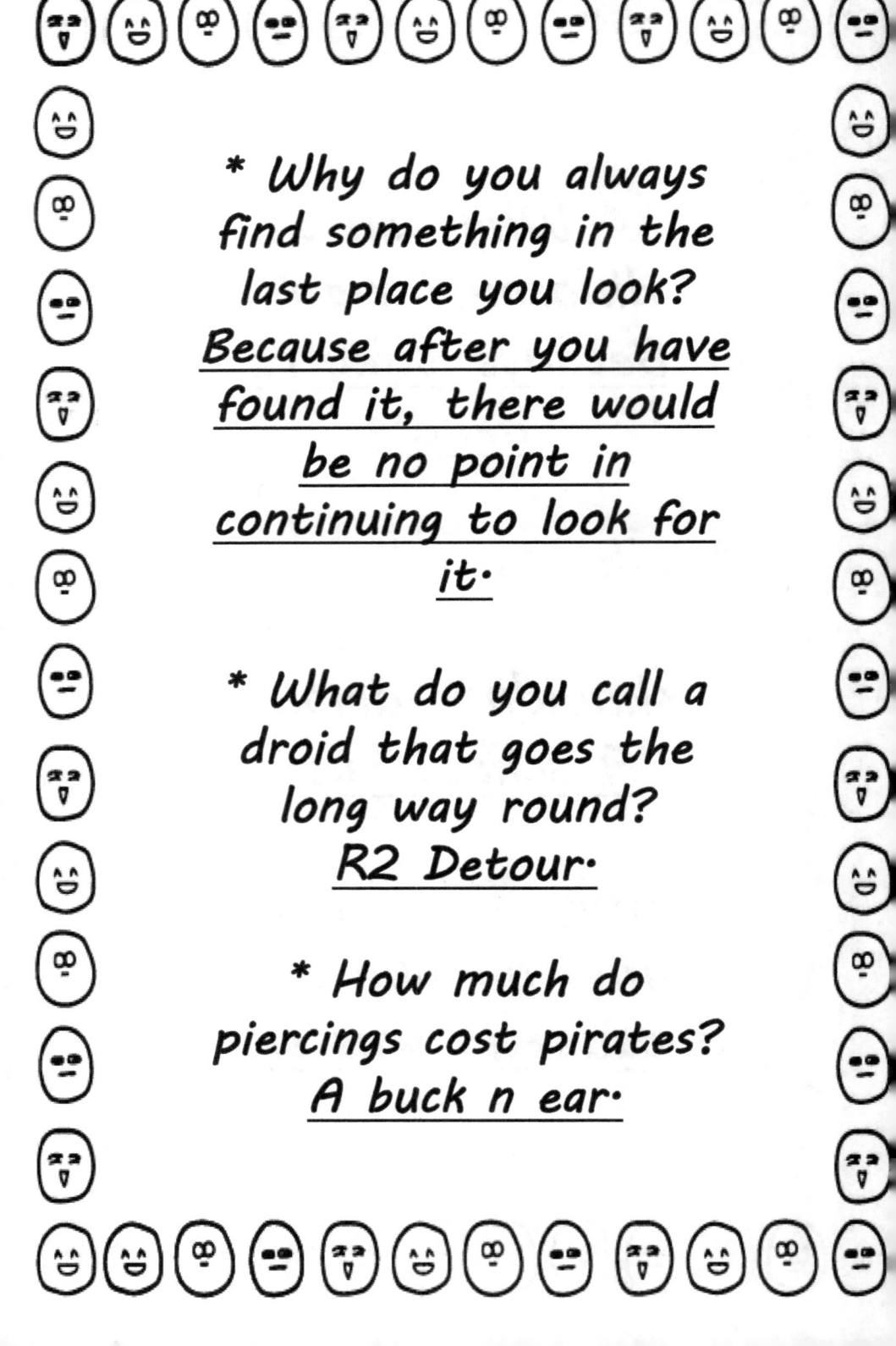

* Why do you always find something in the last place you look? Because after you have found it, there would be no point in continuing to look for it.

* What do you call a droid that goes the long way round? R2 Detour.

* How much do piercings cost pirates? A buck n ear.

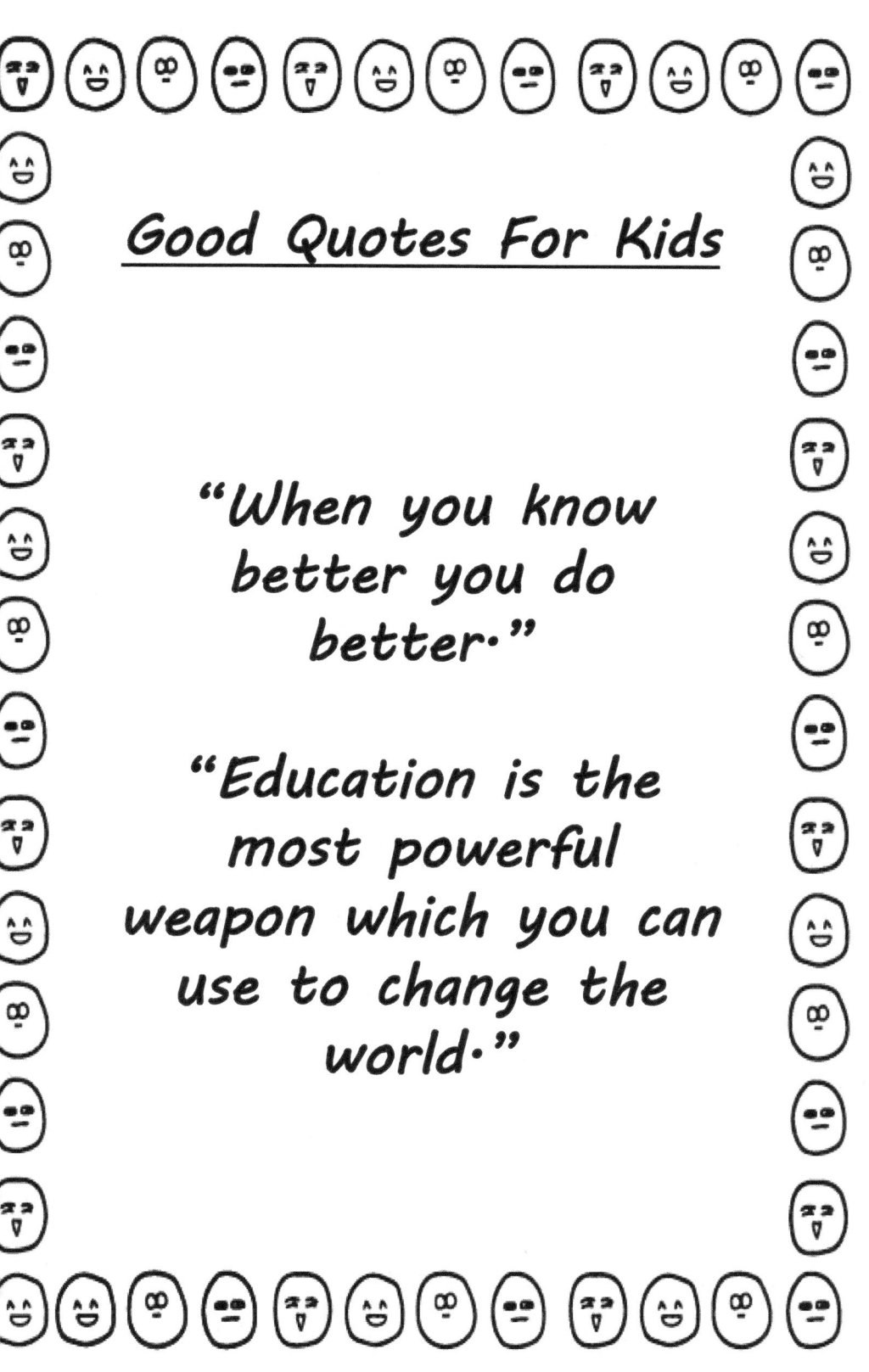

Good Quotes For Kids

"When you know better you do better."

"Education is the most powerful weapon which you can use to change the world."

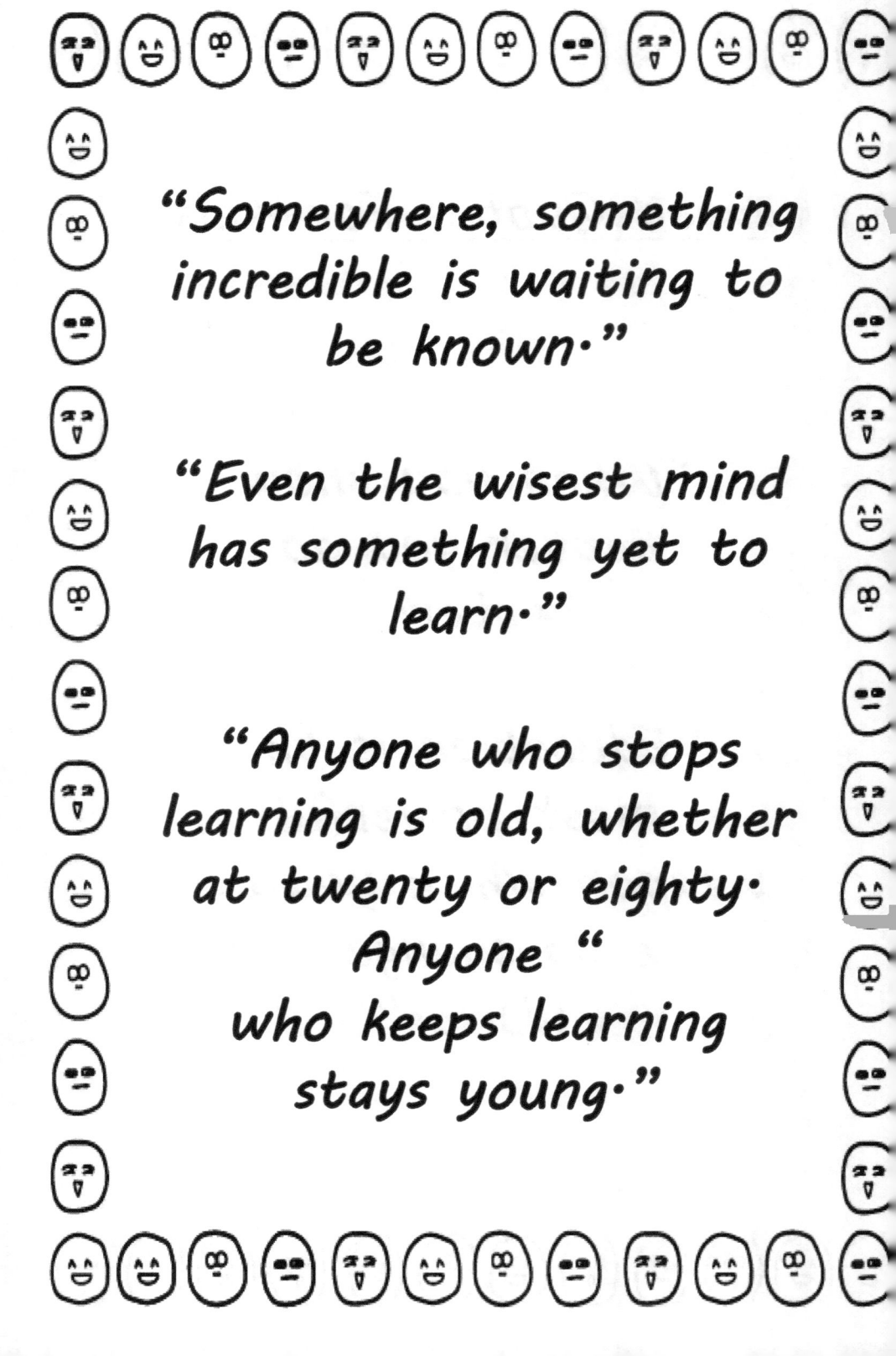

"Somewhere, something incredible is waiting to be known."

"Even the wisest mind has something yet to learn."

"Anyone who stops learning is old, whether at twenty or eighty. Anyone who keeps learning stays young."

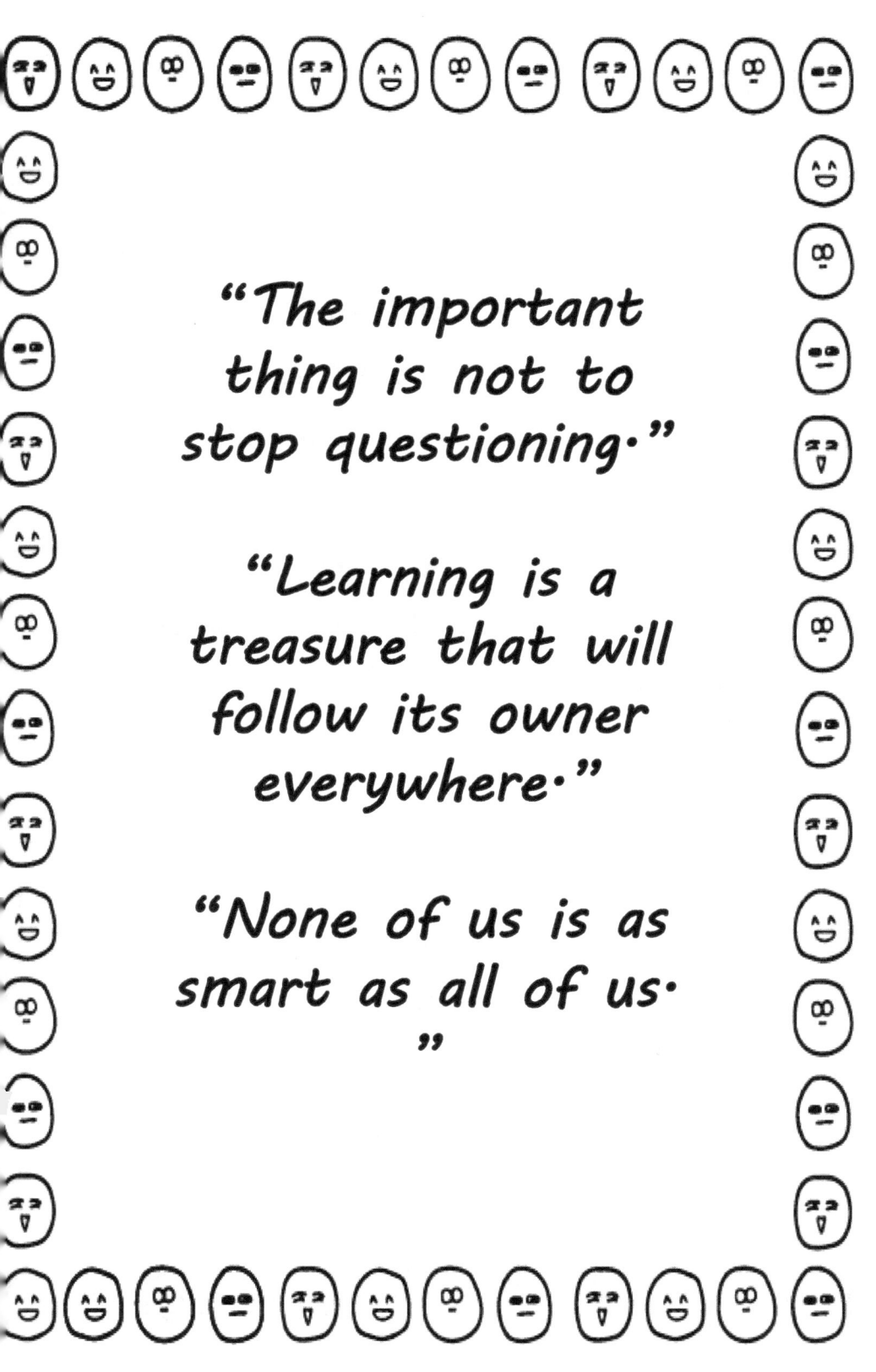

"The important thing is not to stop questioning."

"Learning is a treasure that will follow its owner everywhere."

"None of us is as smart as all of us."

"A house is not a home unless it contains food and fire for the mind as well as the body."

"Educating the mind without educating the heart is no education at all."

"You can tell whether a man is clever by his answers. You can tell whether a man is wise by his questions."

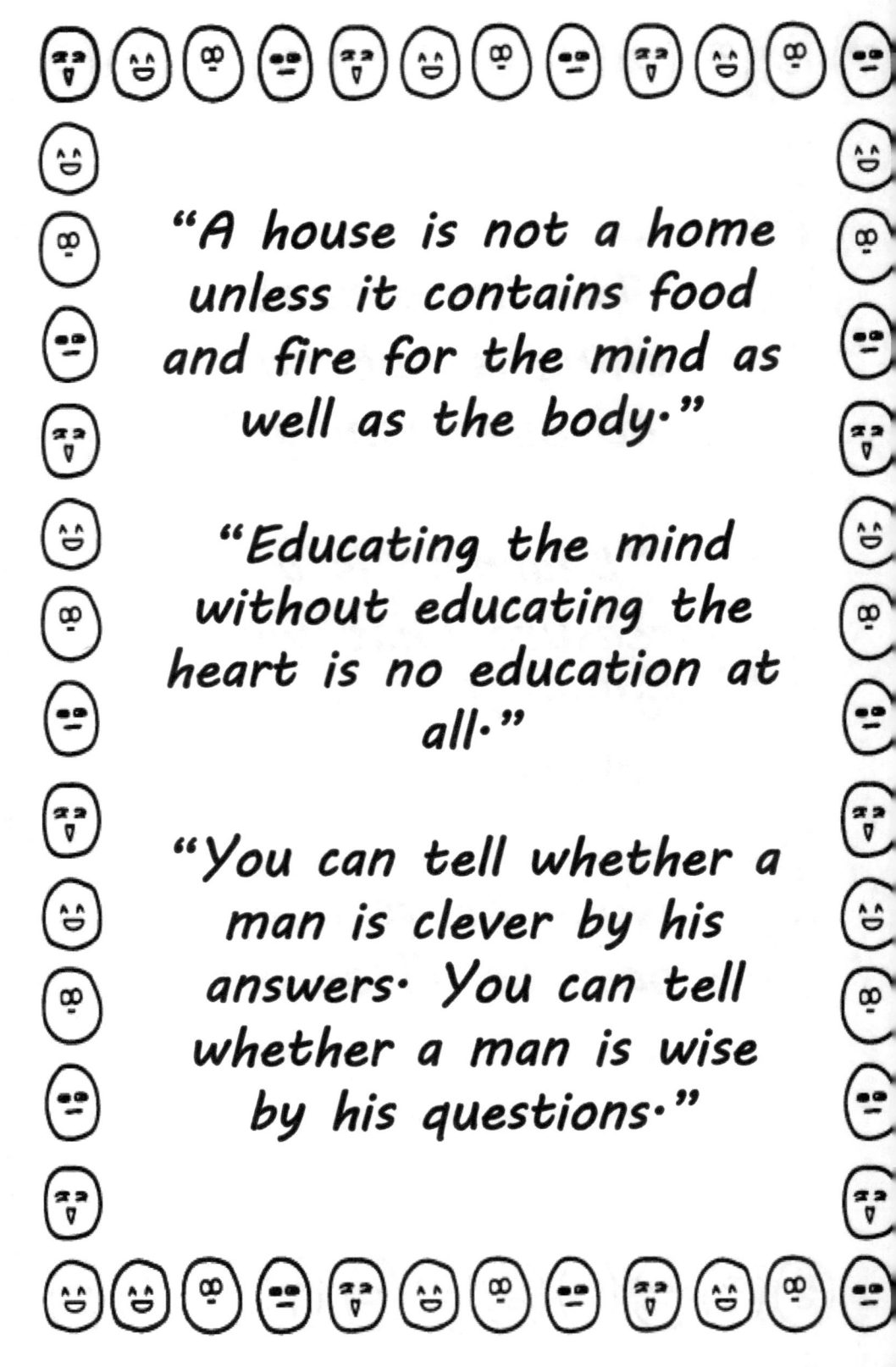

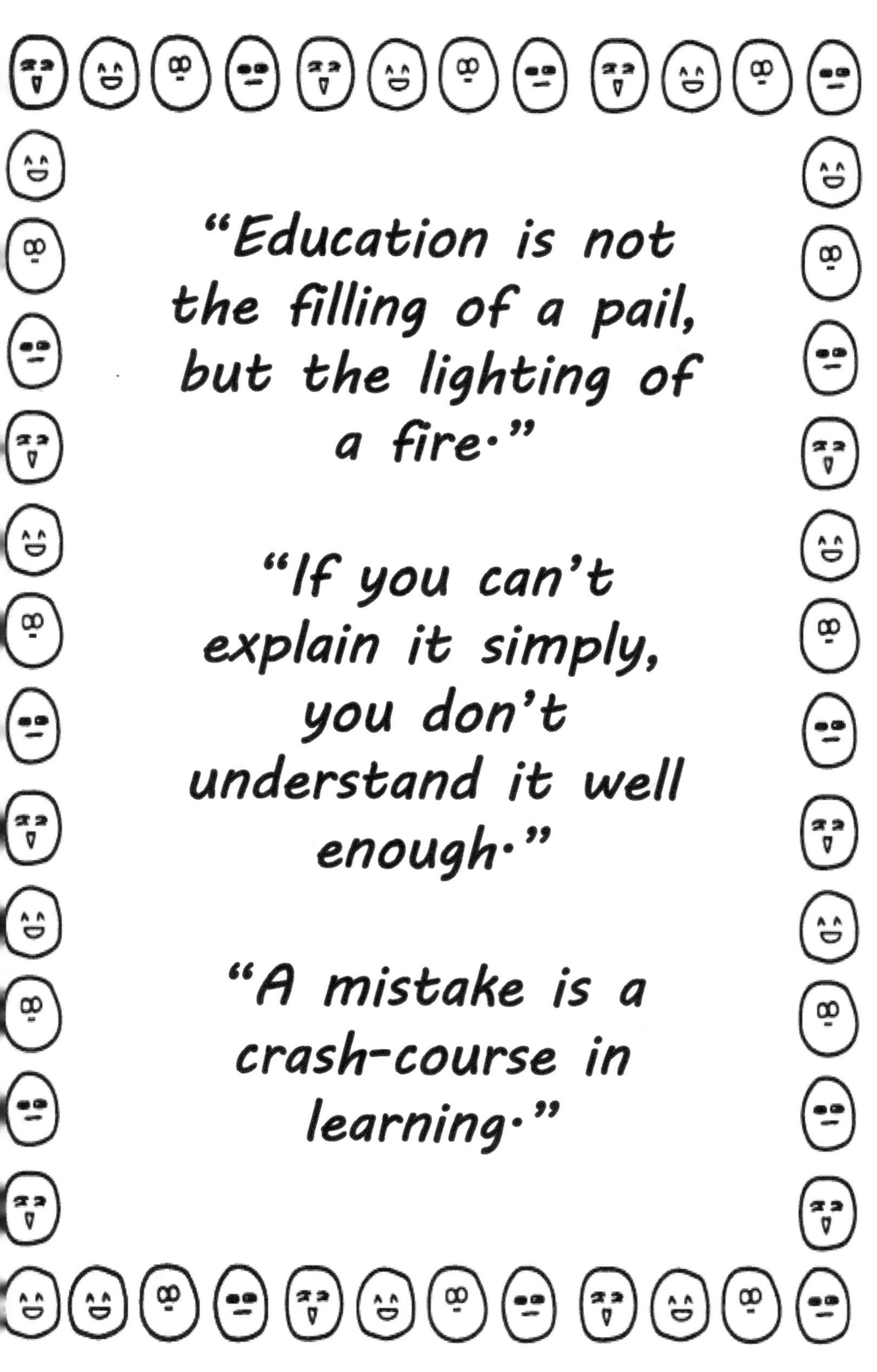

"Education is not the filling of a pail, but the lighting of a fire."

"If you can't explain it simply, you don't understand it well enough."

"A mistake is a crash-course in learning."

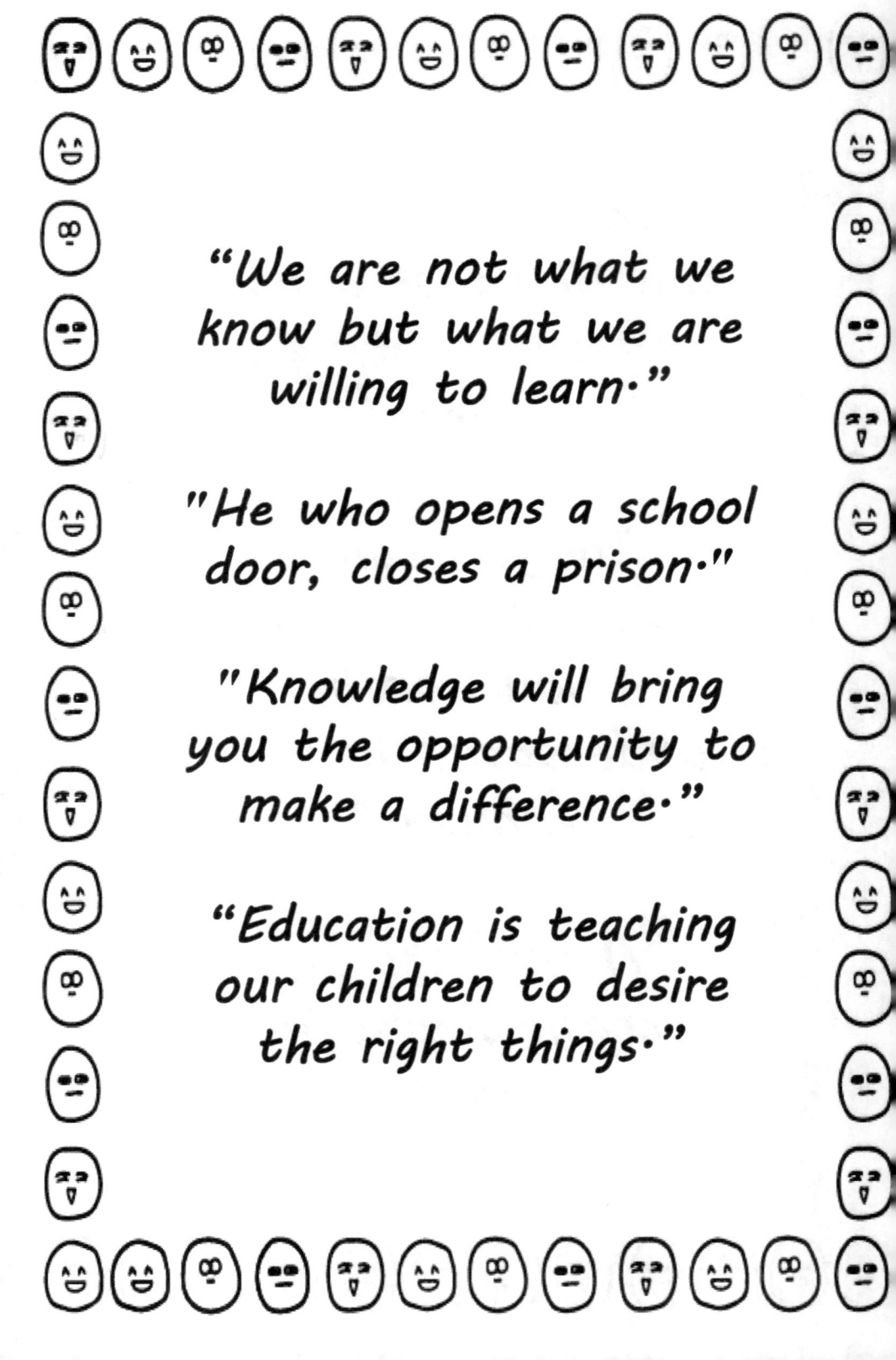

"We are not what we know but what we are willing to learn."

"He who opens a school door, closes a prison."

"Knowledge will bring you the opportunity to make a difference."

"Education is teaching our children to desire the right things."

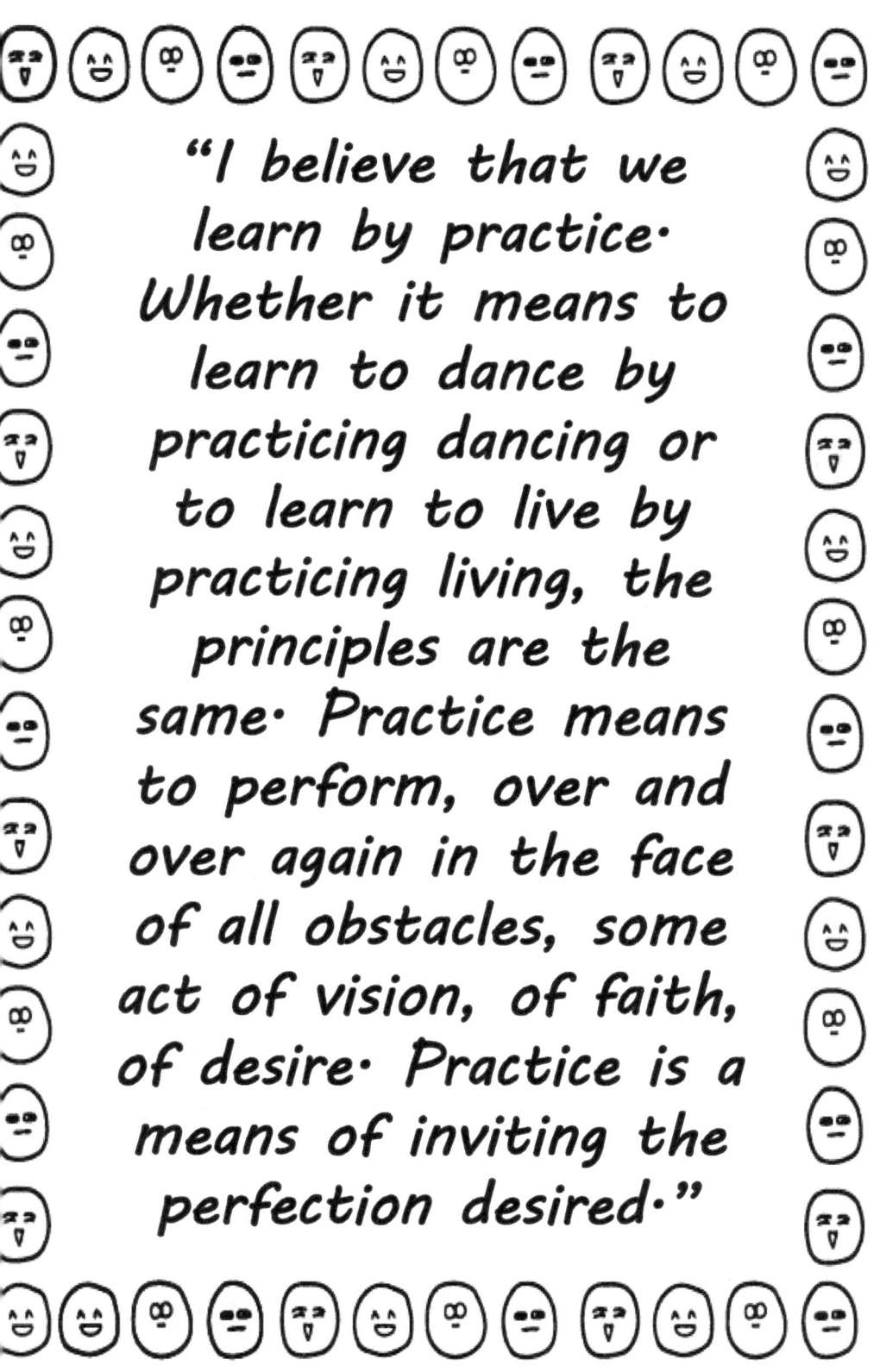

"I believe that we learn by practice. Whether it means to learn to dance by practicing dancing or to learn to live by practicing living, the principles are the same. Practice means to perform, over and over again in the face of all obstacles, some act of vision, of faith, of desire. Practice is a means of inviting the perfection desired."

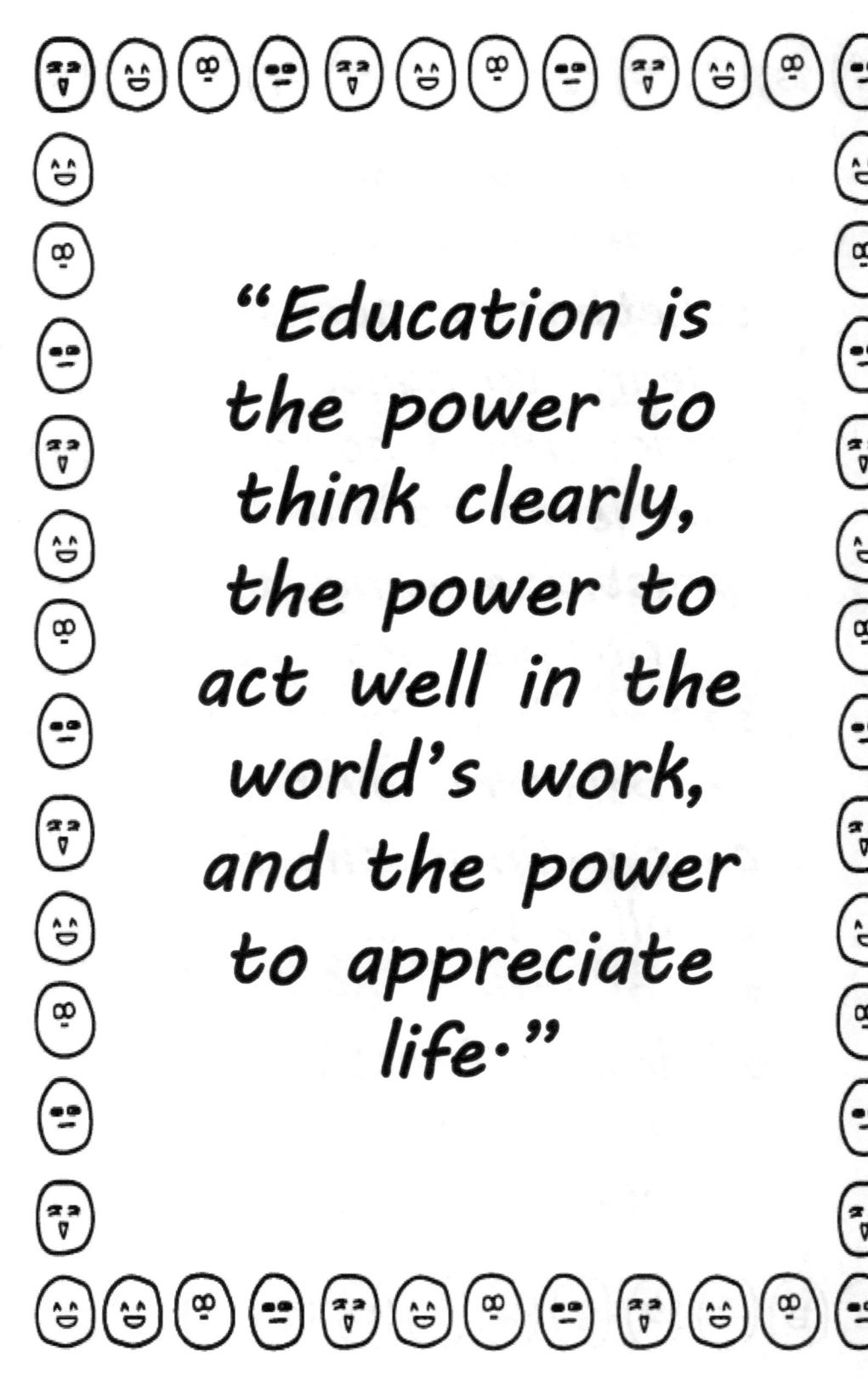

"Education is the power to think clearly, the power to act well in the world's work, and the power to appreciate life."

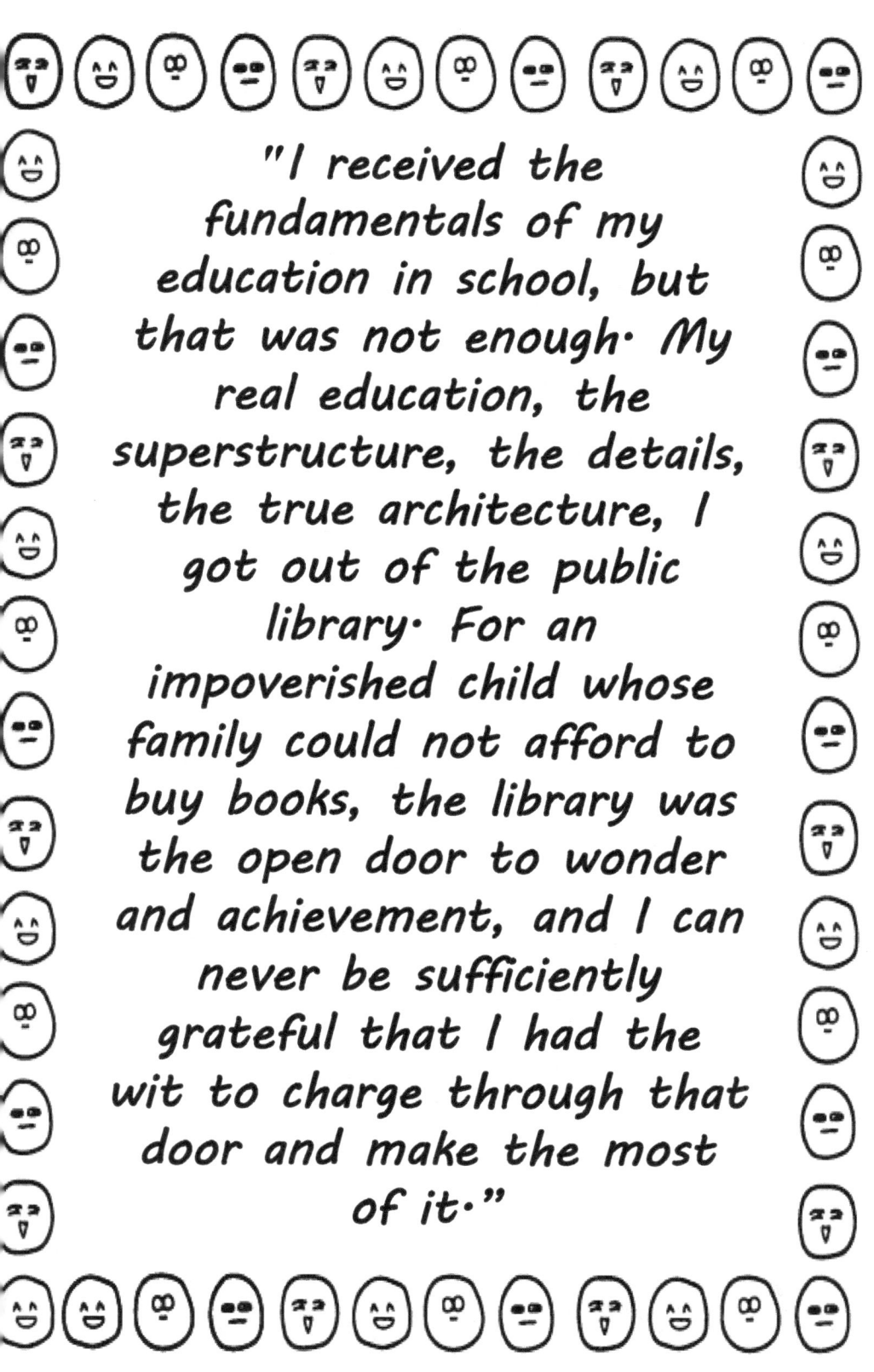

"I received the fundamentals of my education in school, but that was not enough. My real education, the superstructure, the details, the true architecture, I got out of the public library. For an impoverished child whose family could not afford to buy books, the library was the open door to wonder and achievement, and I can never be sufficiently grateful that I had the wit to charge through that door and make the most of it."

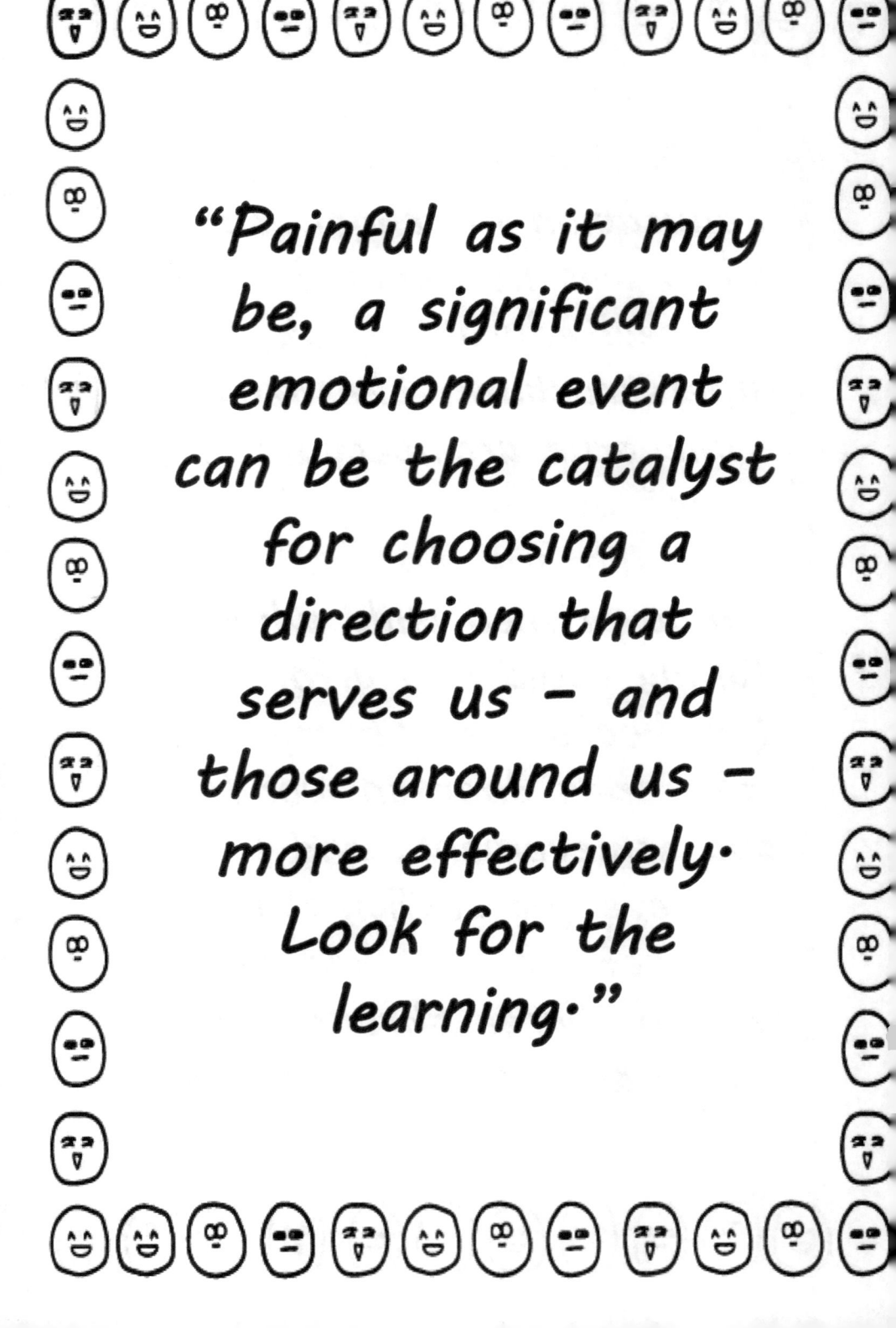

"Painful as it may be, a significant emotional event can be the catalyst for choosing a direction that serves us – and those around us – more effectively. Look for the learning."

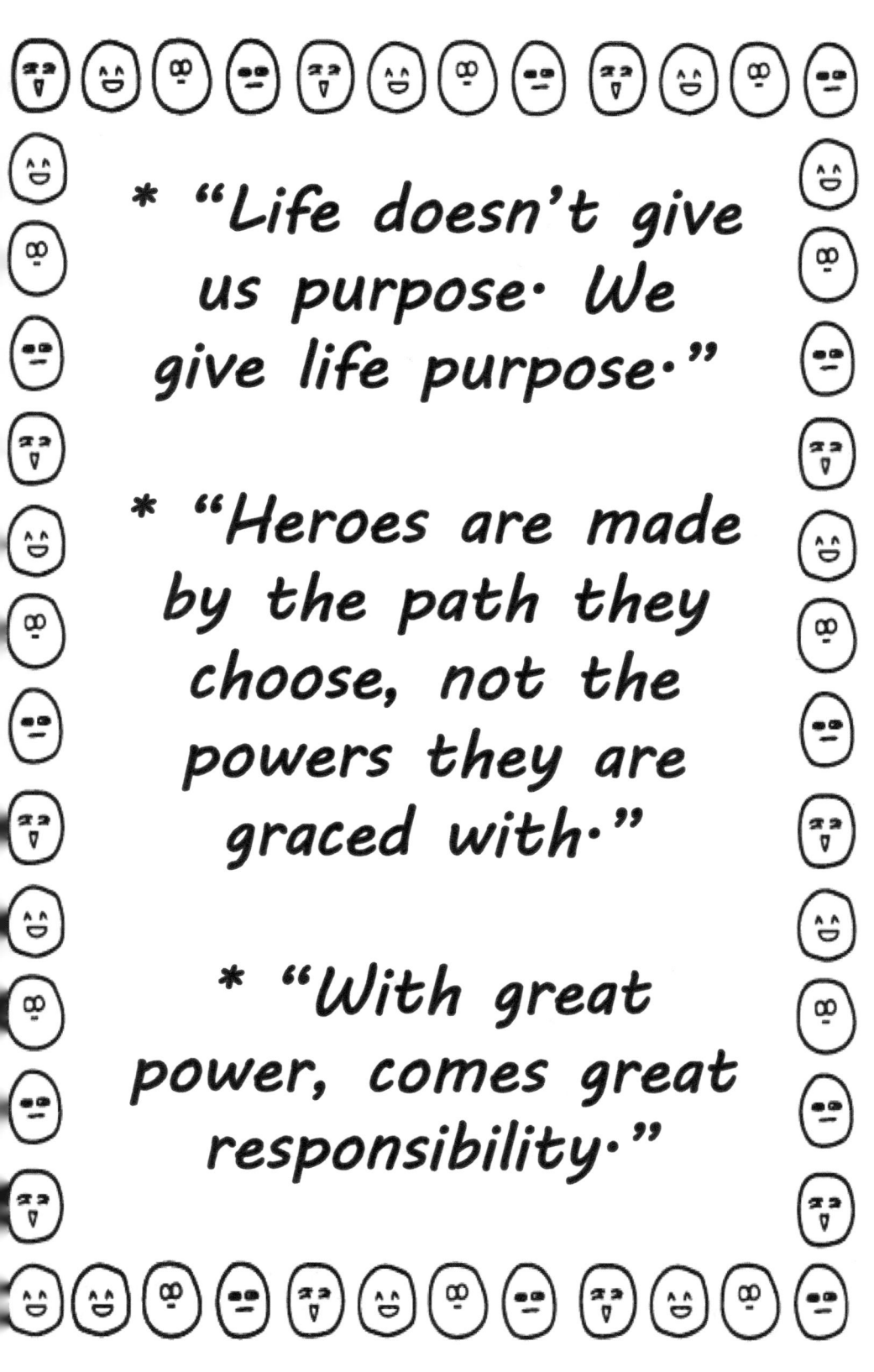

* "Life doesn't give us purpose. We give life purpose."

* "Heroes are made by the path they choose, not the powers they are graced with."

* "With great power, comes great responsibility."

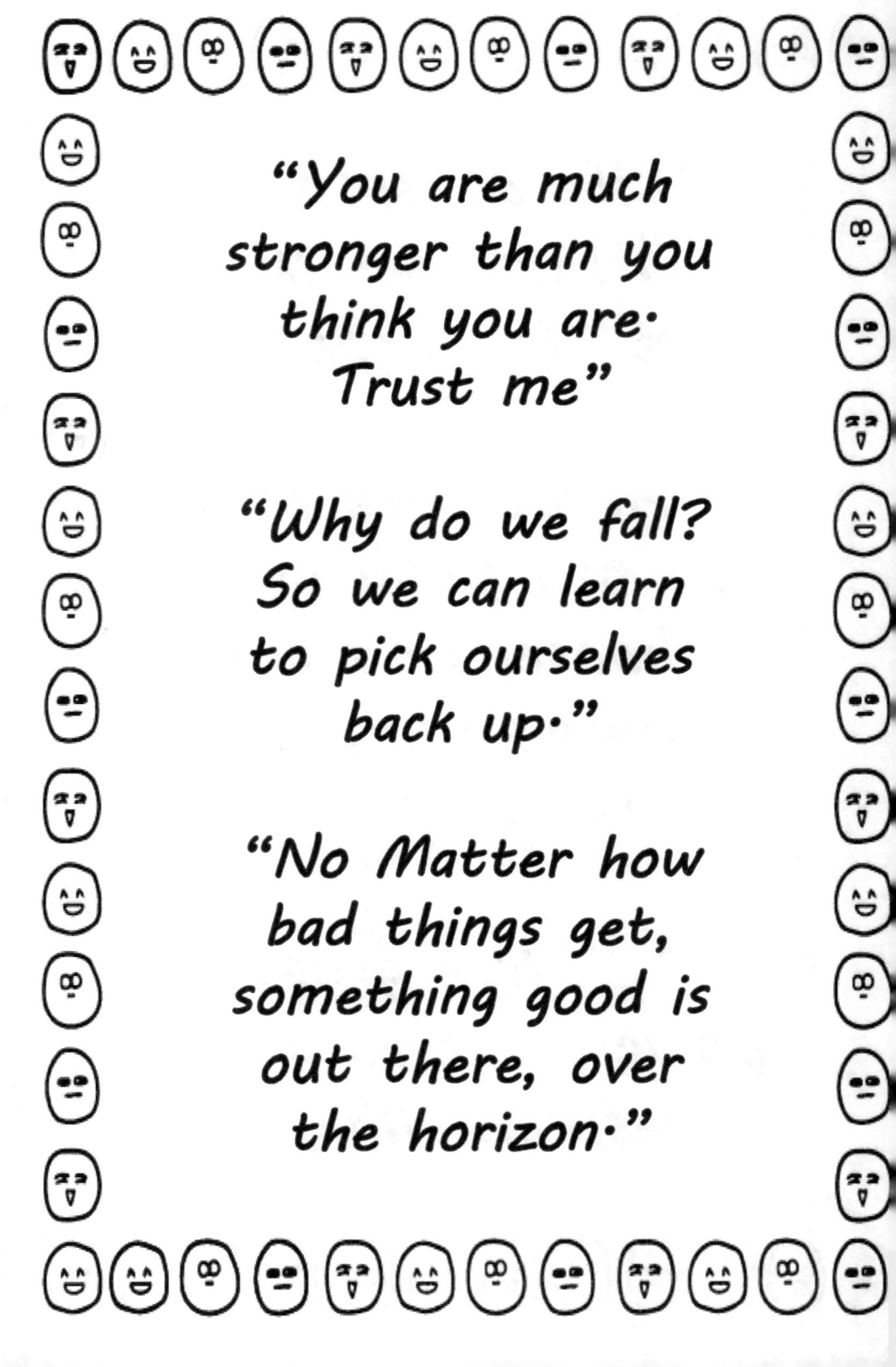

"You are much stronger than you think you are. Trust me"

"Why do we fall? So we can learn to pick ourselves back up."

"No Matter how bad things get, something good is out there, over the horizon."

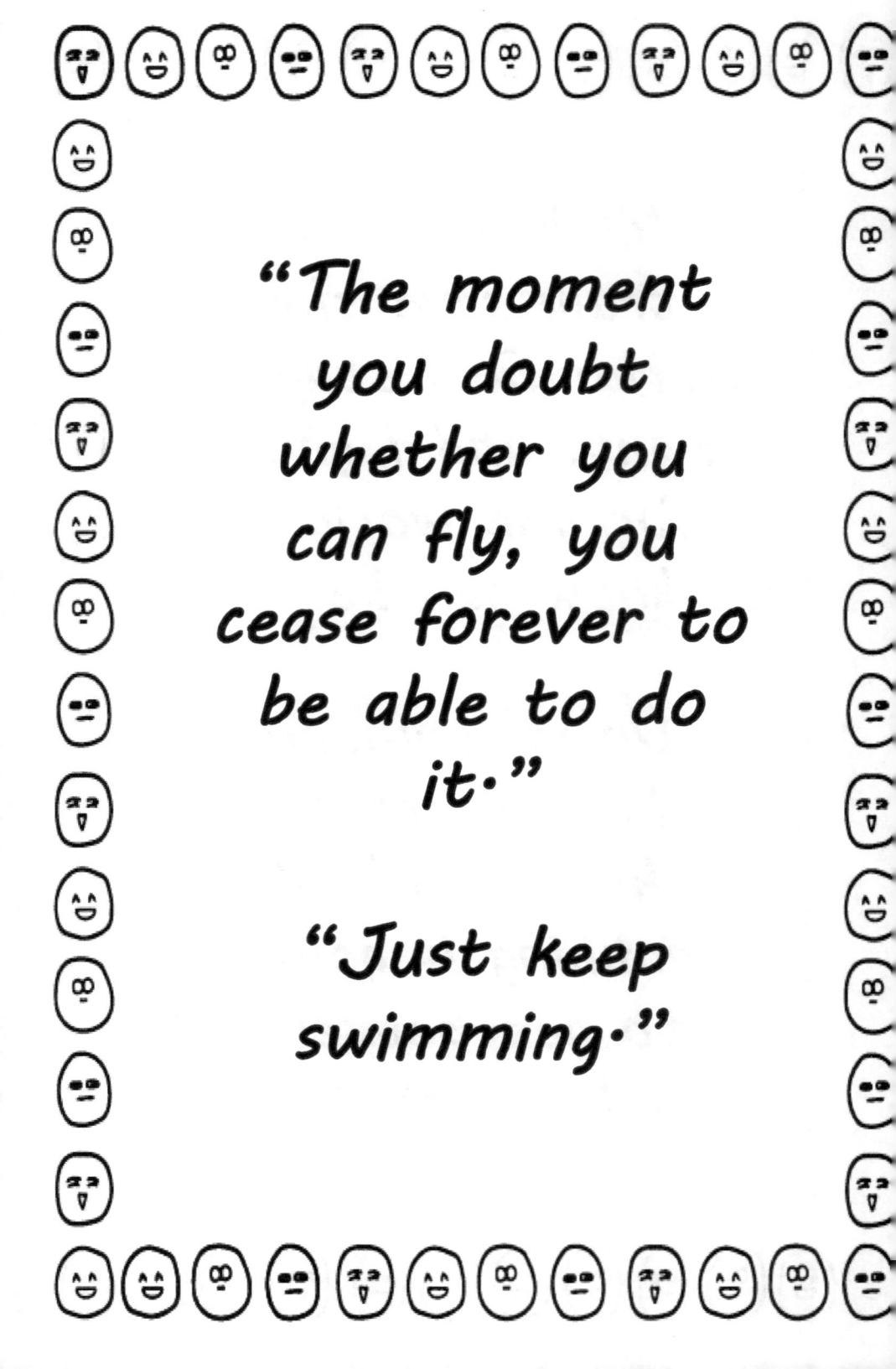

"The moment you doubt whether you can fly, you cease forever to be able to do it."

"Just keep swimming."

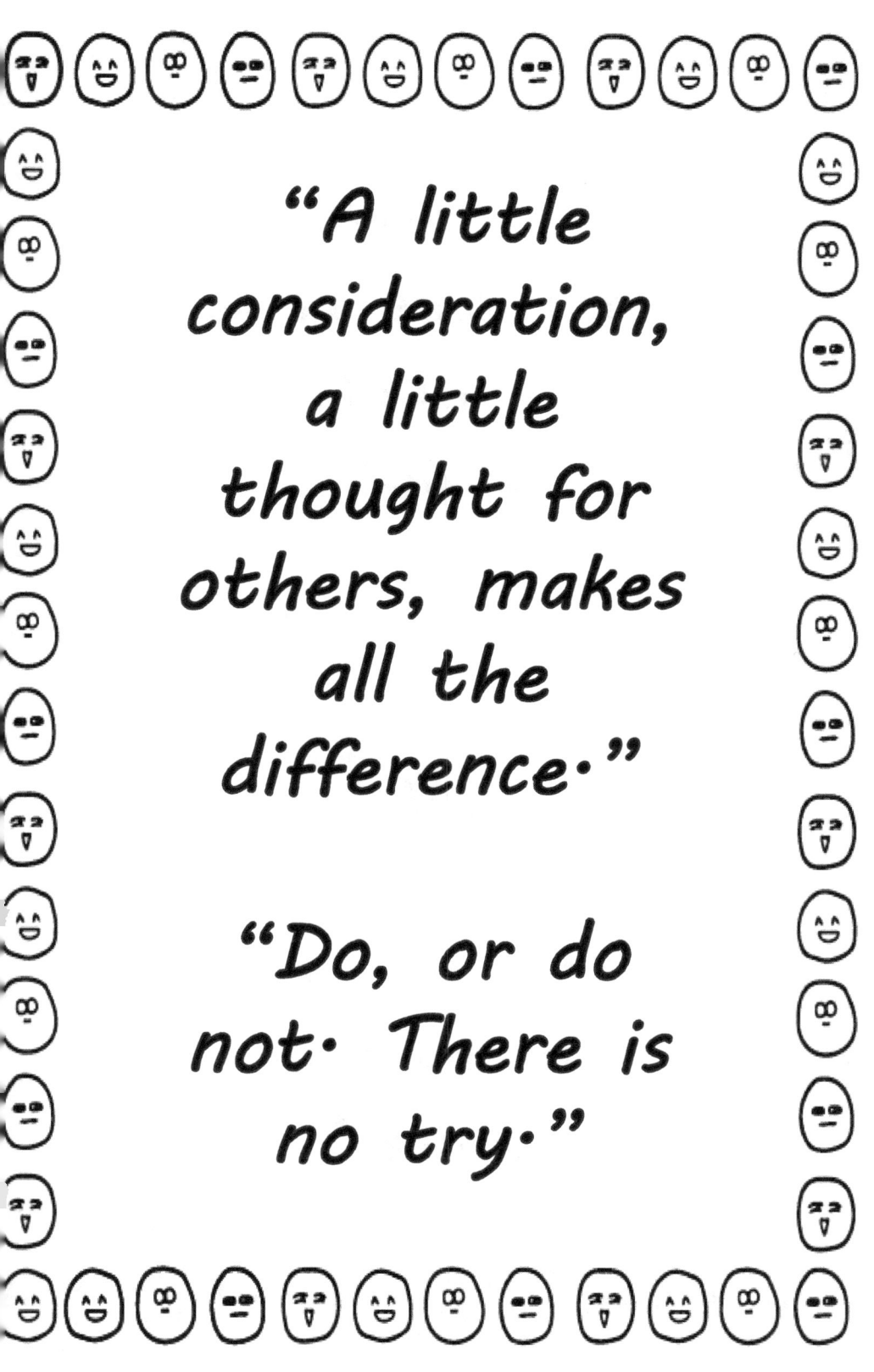

"A little consideration, a little thought for others, makes all the difference."

"Do, or do not. There is no try."

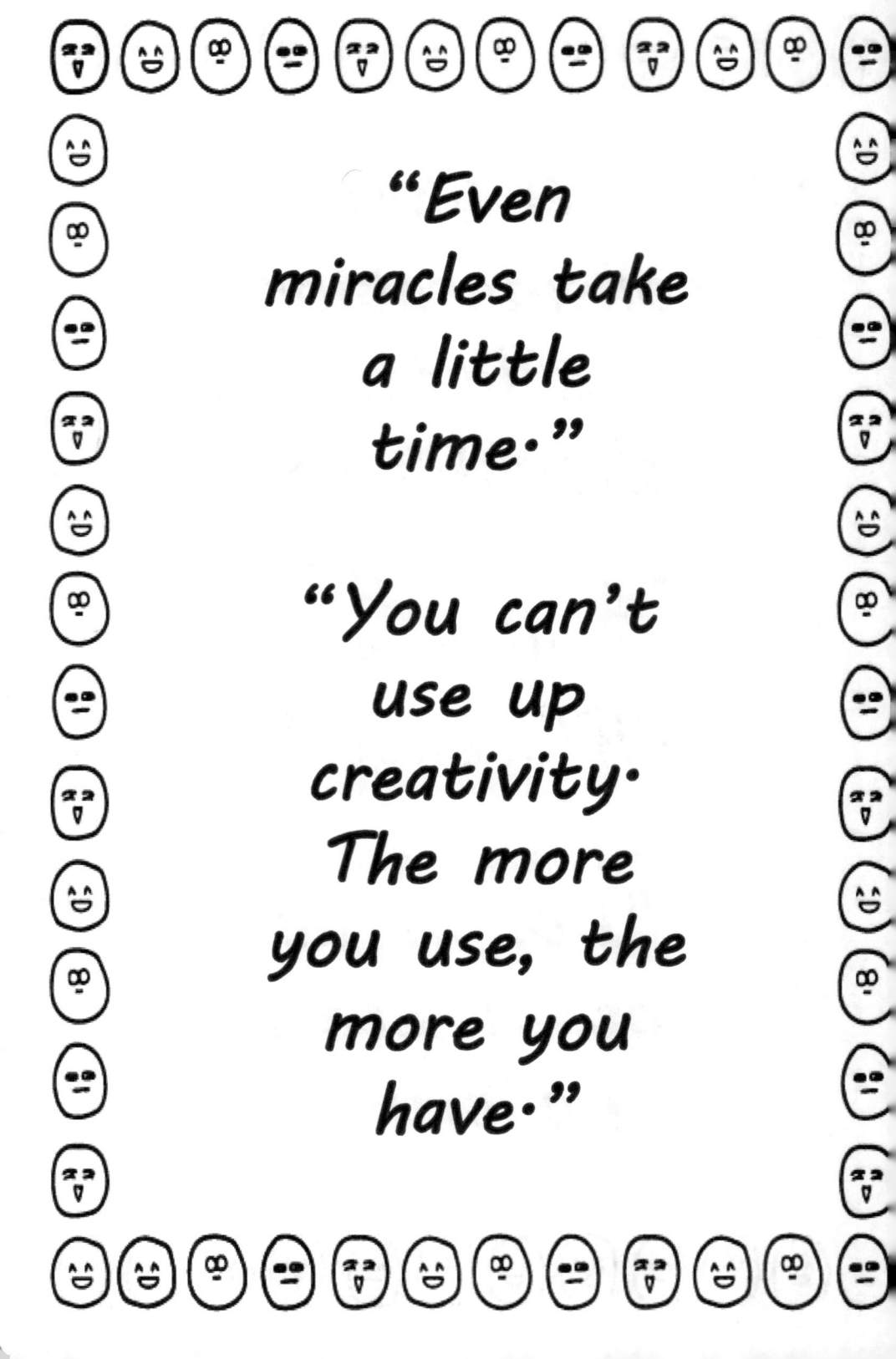

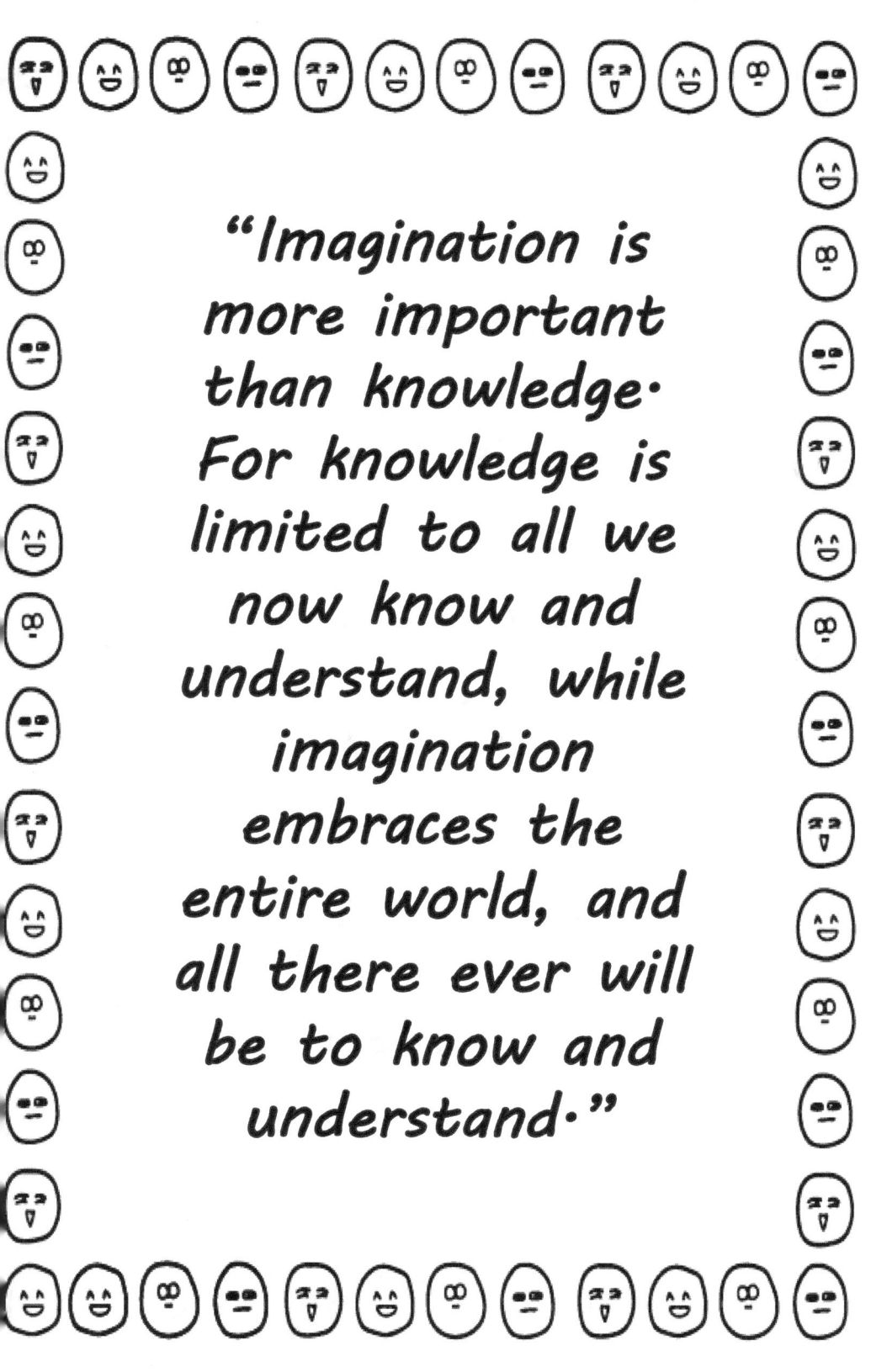

"Imagination is more important than knowledge. For knowledge is limited to all we now know and understand, while imagination embraces the entire world, and all there ever will be to know and understand."

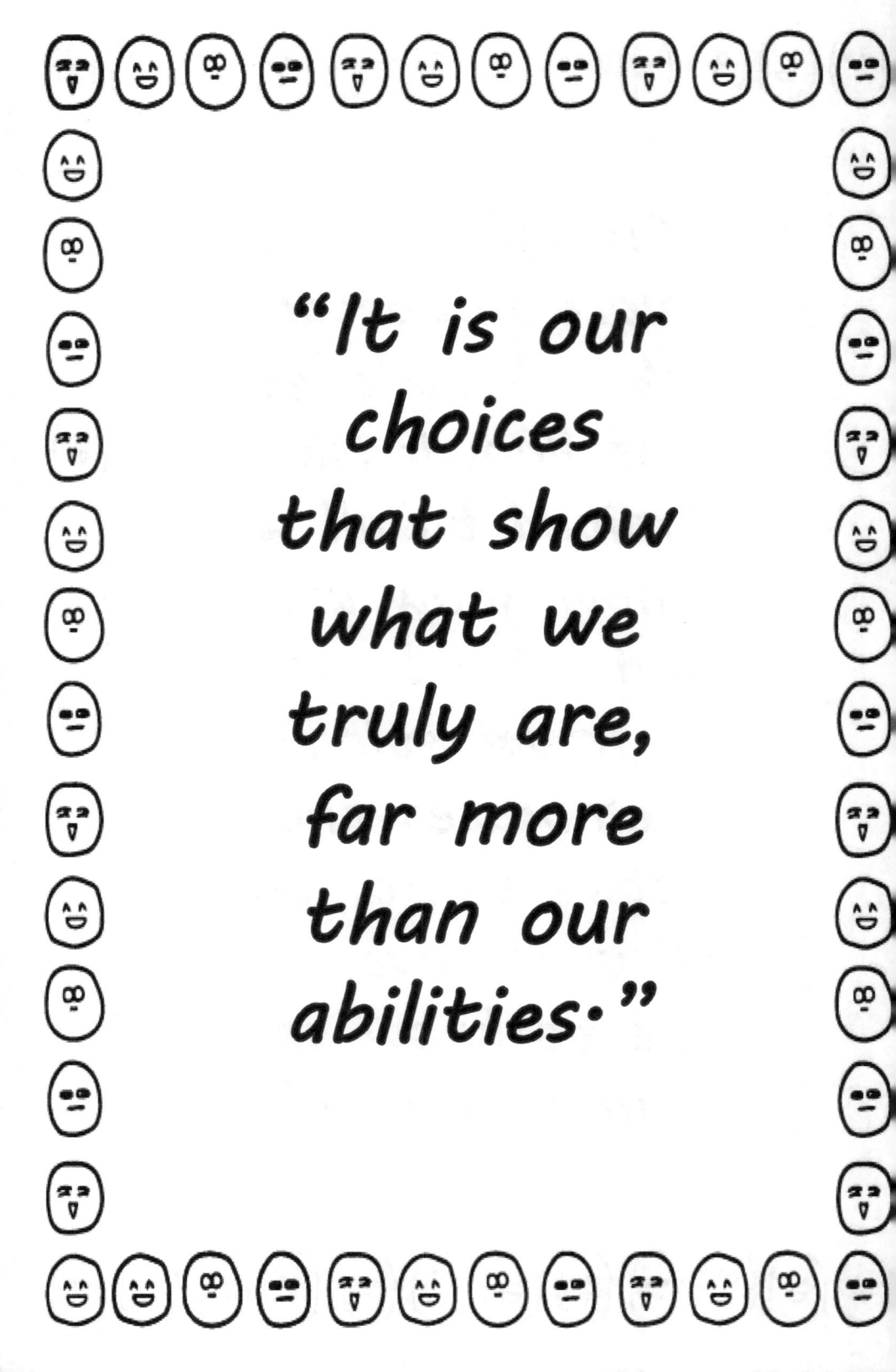

"It is our choices that show what we truly are, far more than our abilities."

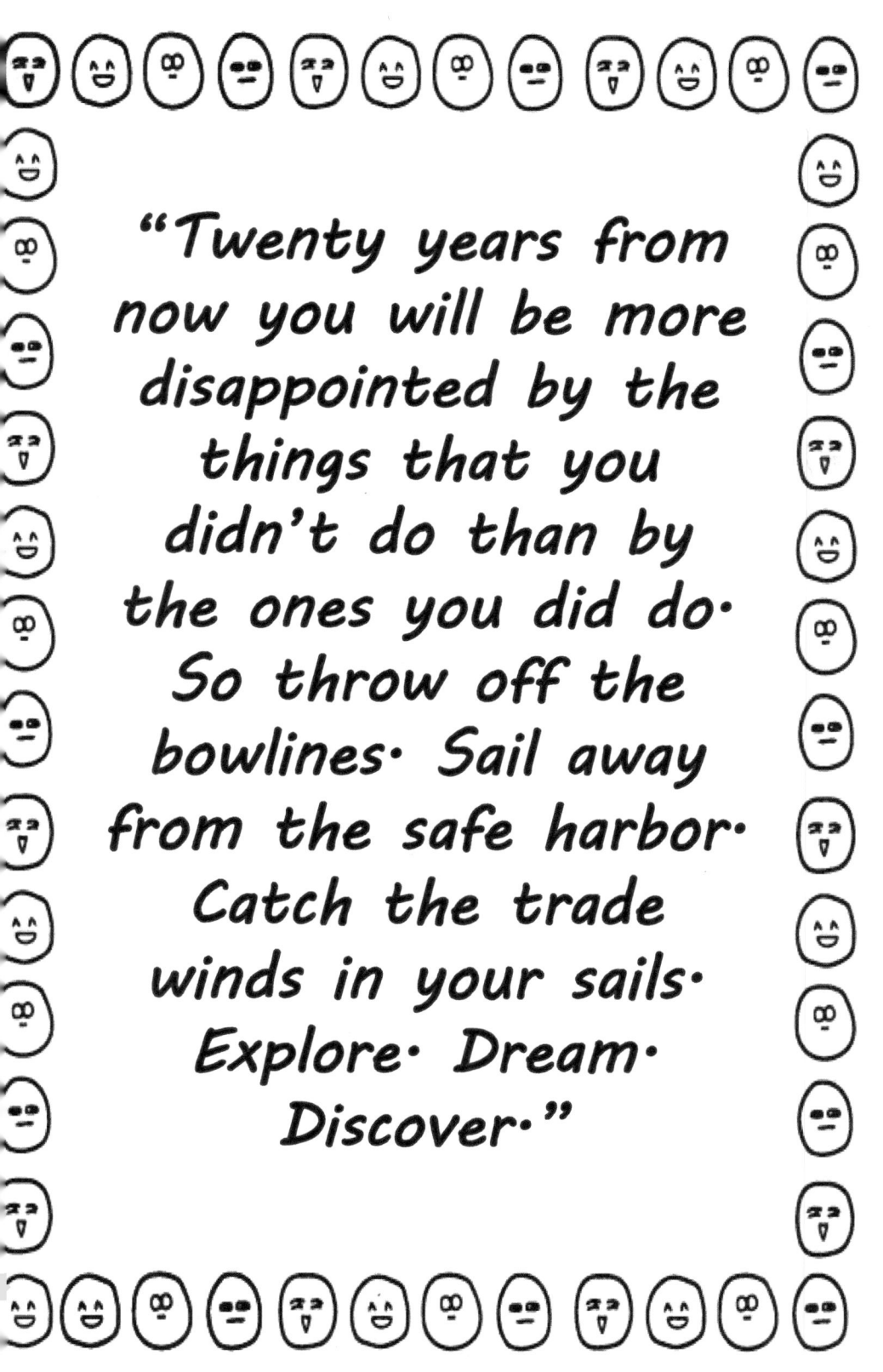

"Twenty years from now you will be more disappointed by the things that you didn't do than by the ones you did do. So throw off the bowlines. Sail away from the safe harbor. Catch the trade winds in your sails. Explore. Dream. Discover."

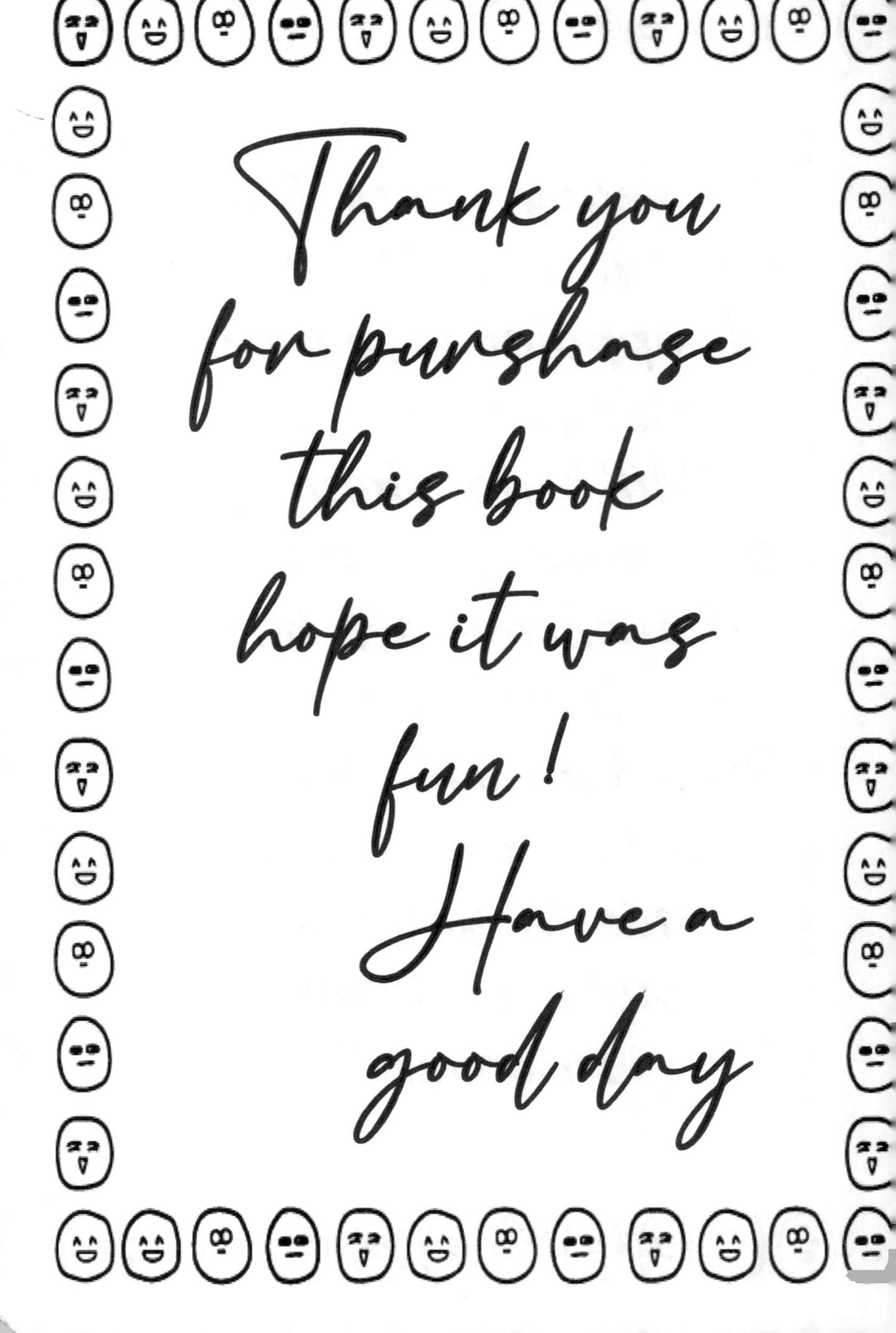

Printed in the USA
CPSIA information can be obtained
at www.ICGtesting.com
LVHW020045311024
795309LV00007B/190